Travels in the Americas

The France Chicago Collection

A series of books translated with the generous support of
the University of Chicago's France Chicago Center

Travels in the Americas

Notes and Impressions of a New World

ALBERT CAMUS

Edited and with an introduction by Alice Kaplan
Translated by Ryan Bloom
Annotated by Alice Kaplan and Ryan Bloom

The University of Chicago Press   *Chicago & London*

The University of Chicago Press, Chicago 60637
The University of Chicago Press, Ltd., London
English translation © Ryan Bloom
Introduction © Alice Kaplan
Published 2023
Printed in the United States of America

32 31 30 29 28 27 26 25 24 23   1 2 3 4 5

ISBN-13: 978-0-226-69495-5 (cloth)
ISBN-13: 978-0-226-75040-8 (e-book)
DOI: https://doi.org/10.7208/chicago/9780226750408.001.0001

Originally published in French as *Journaux de voyage* ©
Éditions GALLIMARD, Paris, 1978.

Library of Congress Cataloging-in-Publication Data

Names: Camus, Albert, 1913–1960, author. | Kaplan, Alice Yaeger, editor. |
Bloom, Ryan, 1980– translator.
Title: Travels in the Americas : notes and impressions of a new world /
Albert Camus ; edited and with an introduction by Alice Kaplan ; translated by
Ryan Bloom ; annotated by Alice Kaplan and Ryan Bloom.
Other titles: France Chicago collection.
Description: Chicago : The University of Chicago Press, 2023. | Series:
The France Chicago collection | Includes bibliographical references and index.
Identifiers: LCCN 2022034896 | ISBN 9780226694955 (cloth) |
ISBN 9780226750408 (ebook)
Subjects: LCSH: Camus, Albert, 1913–1960—Travel—United States. |
Camus, Albert, 1913–1960—Travel—South America. | United States—
Description and travel. | South America—Description and travel.
Classification: LCC PQ2605.A3734 Z46 2023 | DDC 848/.91403—
dc23/eng/20220922
LC record available at https://lccn.loc.gov/2022034896

♾ This paper meets the requirements of ANSI/NISO Z39.48-1992
(Permanence of Paper).

Introduction

Alice Kaplan

These two American journals invite us to travel with Albert
Camus as he discovers the world and to see the Americas, as if
for the first time, through his eyes. The young writer crossed
from Le Havre to New York in March 1946, and from Marseille to Dakar to Rio de Janeiro in July 1949. He visited the
East Coast of the US and Canada on the first four-month trip,
and Brazil, Chile, Uruguay, and Argentina during a packed two-
month tour of South America. Both North and South American diaries recount his adventures from the time his ship
weighs anchor to his return to France. The French have a name
for this kind of observational writing: *choses vues* (things seen).
The travel logs are not confessional diaries, yet their gaze outward opens a large window onto the writer's aspirations and
values.

Camus's world had changed radically from 1946, when he
set off to New York in the euphoria of France's liberation from
Nazi occupation, to 1949, when fame and controversy had be-
gun to weigh on him. When he left for New York he was a literary editor at Gallimard. He had made his mark in France as the
leading editorialist for *Combat*, the daily paper that aspired to
bring the spirit of the Resistance into the postwar world. The
previous fall he had taken a leave from *Combat*, and he was

struggling with revisions of a novel called *The Plague*, whose final form was eluding him. Though *The Stranger* was about to be published in English, very few people in the United States knew yet who Camus was. The New York trip marks his beginnings as an international writer. He sat for a Cecil Beaton photo at *Vogue*, recorded a radio interview with Paul Gilson, was interviewed by Dorothy Norman for her column in the *New York Post*, and celebrated the launch of *The Stranger* on the rooftop of the Astor Hotel. He met the cream of the New York intelligentsia and enjoyed the novelty of a half dozen college campuses: Brooklyn College, Penn, Columbia, Bryn Mawr, Harvard, Vassar. By his second transatlantic trip in 1949 he was a far more famous man, known as one of the fashionable French existentialists, despite his impatience with that label, and as the author of *The Stranger*, *The Myth of Sisyphus*, and the runaway best seller *The Plague*, published in 1947. He would no sooner arrive in a new country than he would be blinded by flashbulbs and surrounded by journalists hounding him with questions about how much of an existentialist he really was.

In *The Plague*, the novel published between the two transatlantic trips, Camus gives a clue about the kinds of travel diaries he likes. Dr. Rieux is a serious chronicler of the epidemic, while his friend Tarrou, in his own notebooks, is drawn to secondary details, to bizarre characters and odd visions of humanity. He's "an historian of what has no history," recording the most absurd details of the lives of random characters—like the man who delights in spitting on cats from his balcony.[1] In these American travel journals, Camus makes the occasional philosophical statement, but he's generally more Tarrou than

---

1 Albert Camus, *The Plague*, trans. Laura Marris (New York: Vintage, 2022), 22–23. See "Anthologies of Insignificance," in Alice Kaplan and Laura Marris, *States of Plague: Reading Albert Camus in a Pandemic* (Chicago: University of Chicago Press, 2022), 91–99.

Rieux. He's amazed by the ad for the New York funeral home that promises, "You die, we do the rest"; by the hideously ugly necktie shop; by the man driving a giraffe in his truck. In Brazil, he gives a scathing portrait of an obese poet who lectures him about French culture and who then, like one of the rats in the first pages of *The Plague*, "gets up, pirouettes, and again falls back into his armchair."

Camus was stimulated by many intellectual encounters: with the psychoanalyst Pierre Rubé, his cabinmate onboard the SS *Oregon*; with the brilliant Argentine intellectual Victoria Ocampo; with the brilliant young *Vogue* intern Patricia Blake; and with the modernist poet Oswald de Andrade, whose *Cannibal Manifesto* disparaged the ruin of Brazil by European culture. He was also bored by official dinners and obligatory good manners. Time and again, when the city seemed too crass, the people indigestible, he turned his gaze to the sea: "I've always been able to make peace with things out at sea, and for a moment the infinite solitude does me good, though I can't help but feel all the world's tears are rolling atop the sea now."[2]

Like so many other White European modernists of his generation, Camus had absorbed an esthetic fascination with so called "primitive cultures" that seemed to promise an escape from the sins of Europe. And thanks in part to articles by Sartre and Jacques-Laurent Bost, reporting for *Combat* and *Le Figaro* in the United States in 1944 and 1945, he was prepared for the postwar spectacle of American racism.

It's impossible to talk about Camus's vision of American racism without a detour through his own origins. This child of Algiers had grown up in a poor neighborhood in a colonial city where Muslim citizens were denied basic rights while the

2 From the South American travel journal, p. 58 below.

signs of a vital Arab culture were written on the cityscape. In the 1930s, he had been part of an artistic movement, "L'école d'Alger," that wanted to affiliate European Algerian artists with French modernism; they eschewed the condescending, folksy orientalism tendencies of so much colonial art and literature. *The Stranger* and *The Plague*, his first two novels, make only the slightest gestures toward the Arab reality of Algiers and Oran. Often dismissed as overly moderate in his views on Algerian nationalism, Camus stayed true to his belief that France needed to reform its colonial policies or lose Algeria. He recruited Muslims for the Communist Party during the brief period of his party membership. He angered the colonial government with his investigative reporting on famine and misery in Kabylia, the mountainous region whose Berber people were often idealized by the French as "noble savages."[3] In 1945, writing in *Combat* about the horrific massacre of Muslim veterans in Sétif, Camus was well aware that discontent with colonial crimes had reached a boiling point, that Algerian independence movements were forming. He knew from experience that French resistance to an Algerian nation would be fierce and violent. Camus would remain sensitive to the demands of Algerian nationalists and their critique of colonial injustice, but an Algeria without France was unimaginable to him. He wanted to believe that equal treatment could unite all the diverse peoples of Algeria—that equality and justice would be enough to break the cycle of poverty and violence. So he endorsed a federated Algeria where Berbers, Arabs, Jews, and Europeans could live together and failed to see that such a solution was no longer viable. The tension between his political ideals of freedom from oppression and his European

3 Albert Camus, "The Misery of Kabylia," *Algerian Chronicles*, trans. Arthur Goldhammer (Cambridge: Harvard University Press, 2013), 23–81.

consciousness—his desire for Algeria to remain his country— traveled with him to the Americas.

The new world offered him a less complicated canvas than either France or Algeria. Here he was an outsider who could observe acts of racism, on the one hand, while enjoying African American culture from a safe distance. In New York, he describes a diplomat from French Martinique who had been sent as a matter of course to live in Harlem with other Blacks. It was the man's first lesson in American racism. Camus duly notes a counterexample: he sees a White man give up his seat on a bus for an old Black woman. The positive example follows the negative, as if Camus needed to believe in the survival of individual acts of dignity in a society where even basic living space was determined by race. Then there is the cultural question. Camus was awed by Maurice Rocco's boogie-woogie piano playing: "The rhythm, the force, the precision of his playing, the way he puts his whole self into it, jumping, dancing, throwing head and hair right and left." He has the impression, he writes, "only Negroes give life, passion, and nostalgia to this country that they colonize in their own way." "Colonize" is a loaded word for an Algerian Frenchman, and it's hard to know if Camus intends it wishfully or ironically—or both.

The race question follows him to Brazil. There, he meets the members of an Afro-Brazilian theater troop who are preparing a production of his play *Caligula*. The head of the troop, Abdias, takes him to a Macumba performance, a hybrid of African and Catholic ritual, "to coax the god down into the body by means of song and dance." Camus realizes he has to combat his own reverse prejudice—"I like Black people *a priori* and am tempted to find qualities in them that they don't have." He's embarrassed by his attitude. He's almost relieved by the ordinary dullness of a Samba dance hall, and he's disappointed by the way the Afro-Brazilian theater troop has staged *Caligula*.

They've made the story of the Roman emperor into a sensual, flirtatious dance—whereas Camus intended Caligula as a murderous tyrant who would remind audiences of Hitler. In Brazil, Hitler is a distant reference.

＊

Camus's official visits contributed to France's urgent cultural mission in the postwar era: Erase the scourge of Vichy, promote French language and culture in North and South America through events featuring writers and scientists capable of drawing large crowds, and in Latin America in particular, compete with the encroachment of English.

These are not willfully political diaries, though politics were an inevitable part of Camus's daily life on the road. When the writer arrived in New York on the SS *Oregon* in March 1946, he was detained for several hours by immigration officials in early Cold War style. He refused to speak until an official from the French Cultural Services came to his rescue. (His host in New York was the great French anthropologist Claude Lévi-Strauss, cultural counselor at the French Embassy.) We know now that the FBI was keeping tabs on him throughout his North American journey, on J. Edgar Hoover's orders, and that in July 1946, after his return to Paris, an agent named Tierney concluded on the last of an eighteen-page report that the writer presented no danger to American society. He was not a communist, he had no desire to overthrow the government or promote anti-American thought. The report added—in what must have been a rebuke to Hoover's anticommunist paranoia—that even French communists were overwhelmed by the task of reconstructing their own country and uninterested in interfering anywhere else.[4]

4 See a page from the report below, p. 28.

The talk Camus gave in New York, at Columbia's McMillin Theater, still resounds today with the force of his commitment to antifascism and his tragic sense of Europe in ashes. Onstage, he was joined by two writers—Vercors and Thimerais—who, with Camus, represented the spirit of the French Resistance. A decade younger than Thimerais and Vercors, Camus, at age thirty-three, was known to the Frenchmen in the room for his editorials in *Combat*.

Imagine the audience that night—a room full of cosmopolitan New York intellectuals. How many had relatives deported from France, who had never returned; how many had made it into exile just in time? How many were veterans of the North African landing or the Liberation of Paris? The Italian activist and writer Nicola Chiaromonte was there—he'd flown in Malraux's squadron in the Spanish Civil War and escaped Europe through Oran, where Camus was his host. Now he was writing for the *New Republic*. Jacques Schiffrin was there too. Forced out of Gallimard (he founded the Pléiade collection) in the wake of the anti-Jewish laws, he'd emigrated with wife and son to New York where he founded Pantheon Books. Victoria Ocampo, a leading light of the Argentine literary scene, who had just published her translation of *Caligula* in her journal *Sur*, was in the audience as well. She introduced herself to Camus after the talk.

It's important to remember that Camus's visit to North America came only nine months after the end of the war in Europe. Whether they were Americans or French in exile, New Yorkers were starved for news from Europe and from France in particular—they'd been cut off from the country and its literature for five years. They wanted to hear about the recovery, but even more, they wanted to know what moral and ethical conclusions could be drawn from what had taken place. That was the topic of Camus's lecture.

Six hundred people were expected at the McMillin Theater; fifteen hundred showed up, crowding into every available
space. Army veterans, in a show of support, came to the lecture carrying copies of *Combat* they had brought home with
them from France. Proceeds from modest ticket sales were supposed to go to a fund for French war orphans, but someone
stole the cash box; Professor Justin O'Brien from the Columbia French Department—Camus's academic sponsor and later
his translator—made an announcement, and people dug into
their pockets to replace the stolen funds. Camus was struck by
the New Yorkers' generosity: "Their hospitality and cordiality
are also like this, immediate and without affectation. This is
what's best about them." His lecture, "The Crisis of Man," was
published in the pages of *Vogue,* and when Camus sat for his
portrait by Cecil Beaton, the spirit of "The Crisis of Man" was
captured on his backlit, upward-looking face.[5] A week after
the Columbia lecture, Knopf would publish the first English
translation of Camus's 1942 novel *The Stranger.* In a full-page
ad placed in *Publisher's Weekly*, Knopf was promising an existentialist revelation.

On both trips, Camus was an official cultural representative of the French government, "a cultural missionary," and
he strained against his diplomatic bubble. He found old
friends and made new ones who were eager to show him "real"
places—a club in the Bowery in New York with Gilson, a ride
to New Jersey with Harald Bromley, the Macumba rituals in
Brazil with Abdias do Nascimento. When he learned that the
Peronist regime in Argentina had banned Margarita Xirgu's
production of his play *The Misunderstanding*, charging it with

5 Albert Camus, "The Crisis of Man," *Vogue* 108, no. 1 (July 1, 1946), 86–87,
in *Speaking Out: Lectures and Speeches, 1937–1958*, trans. Quintin Hoare (New
York: Vintage, 2022).

Camus photographed by Cecil Beaton for *Vogue*, July 1946. © Condé Nast.

atheism, he canceled his official trip to that country. It must have been bitterly disappointing, since publishers in Buenos Aires had just made his first two novels available in Spanish after the Franco regime in Spain had censored them for their supposed anti-Catholic values. (*The Plague* was published in Buenos Aires in 1948; *The Stranger* in July 1949 a month before Camus's visit.) In the place of an official visit, Camus spent three nights as a private citizen as Victoria Ocampo's guest in a mansion he likens in his diary to a plantation house in *Gone with the Wind*.

In Chile, where he spent four days, the country was in an uproar. The government had just outlawed the Communist Party, and communist writer Pablo Neruda was forced into hiding. Because of the protests, Camus couldn't give his scheduled talk at the university, so it was moved to the French Institute. Santiago was in a state of emergency. But Camus didn't stay around the city for the protests against a hike in public transit fares—the famous "chaucha revolt" of August 16. He left with his French hosts for a trip to the mountains.

The curiosity of a writer stunned by bright lights and bottomless larders after five years of wartime deprivation gives the North American diaries a bemused and sometimes incredulous tone. To his new friend Waldo Frank, Camus quips that America has taught him many "negative truths."[6] He hides both the romantic heights of a new love affair and the signs of a new bout of tuberculosis. He refers only to his flu or to a fever that subsides or devours him. We know more, thanks to the reminiscences of his closest companion, a woman whose name never appears in these pages. Patricia Blake, a *Vogue* student intern he met after a lecture and who accompanied him in New York and on the road, talked about symptoms so severe, he would need to be alone. It wasn't difficult to connect her lover's strange fascination with funeral parlors and undertakers and cemeteries to his chronic illness. A literary intellectual who shared Camus's passion for Russian literature, Patricia Blake stayed in touch with Camus for the rest of his life.[7]

6 Albert Camus to Waldo Frank, May 18, 1946, Waldo Frank Papers, University of Pennsylvania Libraries Special Collections, box 5, folder 243. The letter is written from his temporary apartment on Central Park West.

7 On Blake and Camus, see Herbert Lottman, *Albert Camus: A Biography* (New York: Doubleday, 1979), 388–91; Elizabeth Hawes, *Camus: A Romance* (New York: Grove Press, 2009), 106. From Lottman's interview with Blake we learn that Camus was working on *The Plague* in New York and that she typed a section of the manuscript.

The South American diaries speak in a more vulnerable, intimate voice because of an even deeper secret Camus was keeping close to his heart. He had just rekindled a passionate love affair with the Spanish actress Maria Casarès. They had met in 1944, when he and his wife Francine had been separated for two years by the Allied invasion of North Africa. Francine finally got passage to mainland France in 1945, and he and Casarès separated. In June 1948, a chance encounter on the boulevard Saint-Germain led to their passionate reunion. By the time he left for South America in July, he was once again desperately in love and anguished by the prospect of even a few months' separation. In the journals, without saying why, or attributing his feelings to any person, he worries about the mail, which has to catch up with him at each stop, and writes that he suffers from feelings of isolation and melancholy.

Camus's correspondence with Maria Casarès goes hand in hand with his South American travel diaries. The two lovers vowed to share their respective journals once they were reunited. "Until today," he writes on July 5, 1949, "I've only written in my journal—but I've done so faithfully, every evening, finishing the day near you. There is nothing in them but the everyday details of a monotonous life, but everything I've written is for you, directed to you and colored by you."[8]

Both North and South American trips are punctuated by episodes of fever, illness, fatigue, the side effects of Camus's ongoing struggle with tuberculosis. By the end of the South American journey, he is so ill that he feels like he's flying home in a metal coffin. The relapse is serious enough to send him back to the Massif Central for treatment. In September, he

8 Albert Camus and Maria Casarès, *Correspondance, 1944–1959* (Paris: Gallimard, 2017), 115.

writes his former teacher Jean Grenier with a summary of his tour: "I performed an exhausting rodeo that gave me no respite. Right now, all I want to do is sleep and not have to talk. I'm having humanity-indigestion."[9]

What difference did these experiences of North and South America make for Camus's life and work? The man of the theater became a seasoned lecturer, refining themes from *Combat* in lectures like "The Crisis of Man" and "Time of the Murderers."[10] New York cemented an enduring friendship with his editor Blanche Knopf, who went on to publish his subsequent novels, stories, and essays in English translation. He continued a rich correspondence with his old friend Nicola Chiaramonte, recently published. In concert with Chiaramonte, following his New York trip, and based on the ethical agenda set forth in "The Crisis of Man," he joined forces with an American "International Liaison Group" of anti-Stalinist intellectuals and helped form a parallel group in Paris. Much like the future Amnesty International, the short-lived GLI provided material aid and information in support of victims of totalitarianism, refugees, and writers and intellectuals endangered by censorship and imprisonment. After his recovery from the South American trip, Camus presided over the group's dissolution, while continuing his efforts behind the scenes—for example, through his many letters to the French president in support of Algerian freedom fighters condemned to death by French courts.

Where his art is concerned, his trips to the Americas inspired two literary texts. One of his most beautiful personal essays, "The Sea Close By," was the fruit of both transatlantic

9 Albert Camus to Jean Grenier, September 6, 1949, in Camus and Grenier, *Correspondance, 1932–1960* (Paris: Gallimard, 1981), 164, my translation.
10 Both talks are included in *Speaking Out: Lectures and Speeches, 1937–1958*.

crossings; he sketched it en route to New York and wrote new pages from Rio three years later.[11]

Camus's trip to Brazil inspired his only story set in the Americas, "The Growing Stone" (1957, *Exile and the Kingdom*). His travel journal provided him with thick descriptions of the drive through Iguape and the Macumba dance ritual. The central metaphor of "The Growing Stone" is an enormous stone—not the boulder that Sisyphus has to roll up the hill, but a sacrificial stone. A European engineer named D'Arrast—the colonial figure par excellence—meets a ship's cook who explains to him that every year, he gives thanks to the God who saved him from drowning by carrying an enormous stone to a shrine at the church. But that night, the cook is caught up in the local festivities. He dances the night away and squanders his energy. He's unable to carry the stone to its destination. In a gesture of solidarity and empathy, D'Arrast carries the stone in his place. But instead of leaving it at the church, as expected, he takes a detour and deposits the boulder inside the cook's hut. (As in the best-known story in *Exile and the Kingdom*, "The Guest," Camus is interested in the road not taken.) Reaching the poor man's hut, D'Arrast is overcome with joy. The story ends simply: "Sit down with us," the cook's brother says. Together D'Arrast and the natives will contemplate the stone.

It would be easy enough to dismiss "The Growing Stone" as yet another variation on the White savior myth in which D'Arrast can fulfill the cook's mission because he, the White man, has not danced the night away. *Noblesse oblige*. Yet the story suggests that the person truly being saved is not the native. The longing of the engineer to be part of this community,

---

11 Albert Camus, "The Sea Close By," from *Summer*, in *Personal Writings*, trans. Ellen Conroy Kennedy, introduction by Alice Kaplan (New York: Vintage, 2021), 186–97.

to leave "the shame and wrath" of Europe, to live in "liquified time" is palpable. In that sense, the poor Black people of this village are D'Arrast's saviors. Eight years after his return from South America, a disappointed but fervent internationalist, Camus was still captive to a longing which, in the light of the ever-escalating Algerian war, his own ambivalence about Algerian independence, and the bitter controversies of his Parisian life, amounted to a lost illusion: a dream of solidarity across race, class, and nations.

Travels in
North America

March–June 1946

America. Departure. The bit of anxiety that accompanies all departures has passed. On the train, I run into R., a psychiatrist who's going over to make contacts.[1] We'll be sharing a cabin on the boat, which is fine by me, as I find him sharp and friendly. In my compartment: three kids who start out rather boisterous but then settle down, their little maid, their mother—a tall, elegant woman with light-blue eyes—and a blond, a little wisp of a woman, who starts crying right in front of me. An uneventful trip, with one exception. As I'm doing a few favors for the young blond woman, before we've reached Rouen, a tallish woman with flat features and a long animal fur asks me if everyone in our car is going to America. If I'm going there. "Yes." She begs pardon and asks me if she can ask me what I'm going there to do. "Some talks."

"Literary or scientific?"

"Literary."

She gives a real theatrical cry, hand darting to her mouth.

1 Pierre Rubé (1899–1991)—French psychiatrist who shared a cabin with Camus on the SS *Oregon*, later naturalized American. With Kenneth Douglas, Rubé edited a special issue of *Yale French Studies* in 1960, after Camus's death. See their article, "Who Was Albert Camus?"

Application No. 2237

AMERICAN FOREIGN SERVICE

PARIS, FRANCE   Date March 7, 1946

APPLICATION FOR NONIMMIGRANT VISA

I declare that the following statements are true and correct:

Name   Albert CAMUS

Place of birth Mondovi Constantine North Africa Date of birth November 7, 1913

Nationality   French

Travel document Passport No.00679, issued by the Prefecture of Police, Paris
France on January 8, 1946, good for one year
Accompanied by

Present legal residence 17 Rue de l'Universite, Paris, France
(Street, city, and country)

Address (if any) in the United States c/o French Consulate General, New York, N.Y.

Purpose of entry lecture tour in American Universities

Length of stay   two months

I have not previously been refused a visa, deported, or excluded from admission into the United States.
The statements included in my application for registration under the Alien Registration Act, 1940, are hereby
incorporated in and made a part of this application.
I understand that I shall be required to depart from the United States at the end of my temporary sojourn.
I hereby agree that if I am permitted to proceed to the United States I shall do so at my own risk and assume all
responsibility for losses, or damage which may result in the event I should not be permitted to depart from the United
States, or in the event my departure should be delayed.

Albert Camus
(Signature of applicant)

Subscribed and sworn to before me this   7th

day of   March   , 1946.

M. E. OSBORNE
Vice Consul of the United States of America.

Nonimmigration visa No. 2237 issued March 7, 1946 under Section 3(2) of the
Immigration Act of 1924. Service numbers 1360
(1360)
$2.75 = Fr.330.00

1361

Camus's visa application to the United States. © Collection Catherine
et Jean Camus, Fonds Albert Camus, Cité du Livre d'Aix-en-Provence.

Occupation : Writer

Presented a letter from the Ministry for Foreign Affairs, dated March 5, 1946
requesting that a visa should be issued to him.

Jackman, Maine

MAY 2 8 1946   24 under Para.
2
one month

Harry Dolloff

I-94#501296

"Oh!" she says. "How wonderful!" And two seconds later, eyes lowered: "I'm a writer, too, you know."

"Ah!" I say.

"Yes, I'm about to publish a book of poems."

"Very good," I say.

"Yes, I've gotten Rosemonde Gérard to write the preface.[2] She's written a rather beautiful sonnet for me."

"Bravo."

"Of course, it's only my first book, but to have a debut with a preface by Rosemonde Gérard ..."

"Who's the publisher?"

She gives me a name I don't recognize. She explains that the poems are in regular verse "because I'm more the traditional type. The modern, I don't know what you think of it ... but me, I don't like what I don't understand," etc., etc. She gets off in Rouen and offers to post a telegram for me that I want sent back to Paris because I forgot to bring R.'s address in New York.[3] She didn't post it as I haven't received a response.

I meet R. in the dining car and we have lunch sitting across from the little blond wisp who's having trouble cracking her walnuts. When we get to Le Havre, the little wisp, looking completely lost, asks if I might help her. We talk a little while waiting for the bus. She's going to Philadelphia. The bus is a dirty, dusty old police wagon. Le Havre, with its vast fields of rubble. The air is calm. When we arrive at the *Oregon*, I realize it's a cargo ship, a big cargo ship, but a cargo ship nonetheless. Cus-

2 The tall woman from Rouen who conversed with Camus on the train to Le Havre was Eliette Boulen (1903–97), author of the 1946 *Montcalm: 1945, sonnet-préface de Rosemonde Gérard*. Rosemonde Gérard (1871–1953), who contributed her preface in the form of a sonnet, was a French poet and playwright.

3 This "R." likely refers to Régine Junier, not Pierre Rubé (see p. 30n11 below).

toms, exchange, a police checkpoint with a little box of cards that one cop consults while another calls out your name—and that I know well thanks to a few cold sweats that boxes like this one gave me during the Occupation. And then we board.

The four-person cabin, with a shower and bathroom, has been turned into a five-person cabin, where it's impossible to sneeze without knocking something over. We're asked to head to the dining room to see the maître d', but what we really see is a comedy routine. The maître d' looks like one of those Frenchmen you see in American movies, on top of which he's afflicted with a number of tics that have him throwing winks and glances left and right. He's trying his best to arrange the tables harmoniously, consulting a layout he has, as all good maître d's do, that lists the titles of some of the notable passengers. Naturally, he wants to put me with another journalist who's on board. I emphatically refuse, and in the end he puts me with R. and the little blond wisp, whose name, O wonder, is Jeanne Lorette.[4] She's an elegant Parisienne who's in the perfume business and who was crying this morning because she'd just left her twin sister behind and because her sister is her whole world, though she's headed to Philadelphia now to reunite with an American man she's engaged to marry. R. is delighted by Lorette's lack of affectation, her discretion, and kindness. I am, too. We're a little less delighted with the cabin. The cot in the middle of the room is occupied by an old man,

---

4 Jeanne Lorette (1910–?)—Camus's fellow passenger on SS *Oregon*, who was traveling to the US to join her American fiancé in Bryn Mawr, Pennsylvania. List or Manifest of Alien Passengers for the United States, SS *Oregon*, sailing from Le Havre, March 11, 1946, arriving New York March 25, 1946. Consulted on the www.ancestrylibrary.com database, "New York, U.S. Arriving Passenger and Crew Lists 1820–1957." Referred to subsequently as "SS *Oregon* Passenger List."

about 70. On the bunk above mine there's a middle-aged guy, a businessman, I assume. Above R. is a vice-consul who's on his way to Shanghai and who has an open, loud quality about him. We settle in, and I decide to get to work.

At dinner, I meet R., Lorette, the tall woman from the compartment (she's not so tall—rather slim and elegant), and a Mexican couple who are "in business."[5] The two women seem to regard our Lorette with a little suspicion. But she's so naturally at ease that she's the one who comes off as having more class. She tells us that her mother-in-law, who doesn't even know her, writes her the nicest letters and that it seems mothers-in-law in America are of truly superior quality. Her fiancé is very religious, doesn't drink or smoke. He asked her to take confession before leaving. The morning of the departure (she'd been getting things in order in the days leading up to it), she woke at six in the morning to go to church, but it was closed and the train was leaving early. She'll have to take confession when she gets there, and, she says in her slight Parisian accent (usually, she doesn't enunciate her words very clearly and she speaks very quickly and you have to lean in to catch what she's saying), "Anyway, I prefer it this way, because they won't understand me very well over there and so they'll give me absolution." We explain that absolution is always given in such cases. "Even for mortal sins." Of course, R. says, certain it's true. We point out that there's probably a chaplain aboard the ship.

By the end of dinner, R. and I agree that our charming Lorette is trying to calm her apprehension by presenting to others, and so to herself, a comforting image of her situation—which may in fact be comforting, but that's beside the point. Either

5 Edmundo Detchart-Dartayet (1898–1987) and Margarita Berriozabal de Detchart (1901–1970). SS *Oregon* Passenger List.

way, we both wish this droll little creature all the happiness she deserves. Getting to sleep takes a little more work. The cabin's about as roomy as a barracks. The old man and the business-man are both snorers. What's more, R. and I had opened the porthole but the old man closed it during the night. I feel like I'm breathing other people's breath and have a furious desire to go sleep up on deck. Only the thought of the cold keeps me from doing so. Wake up at 7:30 because breakfast is served only until 8:30. Work in the morning. Lunch at 12:15. The Mexican man tells me he represents French perfumeries in Mexico City and he praises French quality. The handsome, pale eyes in front of me lose a bit of their pride, and it's clear now that it came mostly from shyness. Lorette assures us she'll never let anyone in her family speak ill of France. She draws us a remarkable portrait of Antwerpian judgment. (If they buy a piece of jewelry for their wife, it's an uncut diamond, never a finely crafted ring. That way, they'll have capital. Fur coats, too. Safe bets, either way.)

In the afternoon, we talk with the vice-consul. I'm not so surprised to learn he's from Oran. Naturally, we give each other a couple of slaps on the shoulder. He's been to the most incred-ible countries, one being Bolivia, which he speaks of highly. La Paz is 4,000 meters above sea level. Automobiles lose 40% of their power, tennis balls barely bounce, and horses jump only over short obstacles. He kept his strength up by eating garlic. His wife, a witty Polish woman, tells R. stories filled with magic. 3:00 P.M. Departure. The sea is beautiful. A sailor's wife, in full lamentation, runs awkwardly along the length of the jetty, following the boat and waving goodbye. The last im-age of France is one of destroyed buildings hanging on the very edge of that wounded earth.

Off to work. At dinner, the Mexican man tells stories about

going through customs. Only one is interesting: the case of an American who had a leg amputated in Mexico City after an accident and who wanted to bring his deceased leg back with him in a crystal box. Three days of discussion to determine if the thing fell into the category of objects prohibited in order to protect against epidemics. Then the American declared that he wouldn't leave his leg behind and that he'd rather stay with it in Mexico, and the United States, well, they didn't want to lose an upstanding citizen. Our Lorette coughs a lot and is worried about seasickness. R. wants to try to cure her with a course of autosuggestion. He does so quite deftly. After dinner, I have a drink with Mme. D., the tall, pale-eyed woman. Husband at the embassy in Washington.[6]

*

Tuesday, 10 A.M. A good night, if short. It's raining this morning and the seas are getting rough. The bar is practically empty. I work in peace. The Atlantic is the color of pigeon wings. I lie down before lunch, feeling a little nauseated, and sleep for a full half hour before waking up fresh as a daisy. Some abstentions at lunch. Our Lorette doesn't leave her berth all day. The Mexican couple leaves the table before the end of the meal. Mme. Douteau, R., and I enjoy a friendly chat. Then R. goes off to bed, looking a little green. Although feeling fine, I decide to do the same. My head's too foggy to work. But I'll read a little *War and Peace.* How I would have been in love with Natasha!

The day dragged on from there, heavy and monotonous. After dinner, the furrier from Revillon tells me about Eastern wis-

6 "Mme. D," mentioned below by her full name, Paule Douteau (1913–?), traveled on a diplomatic passport with her three children to join her husband, Robert Douteau (1906–97), who was posted at the French Embassy in Washington. SS *Oregon* Passenger list.

dom.[7] It's the type of conversation I've never been able to bear for more than five minutes. I go to bed with Natasha Rostov.

*

Wednesday. Get up with a fever and slightly sore throat. A beautiful sun, despite the choppy sea. I spend the morning stretched out in the sun. In the afternoon, English with R. on deck and cocktails at the captain's with Mme. D. After dinner, R. recounts stories of his time as a doctor. Dachau. The pile of dying people, diarrhea running all over each other.

*

Thursday. Rough day with chills from the flu. A little champagne in the evening with R. and Mme. D. revives me. But my head is empty. English in the afternoon all the same.

*

Friday. The flu is subsiding. But life's still monotonous. I work a little in the morning. The sea's still rough. In the afternoon, we receive Mme. D. and L. in our cabin, along with the consul (Dahoui).[8] Enjoyable chat. The consul recounts (with Algerian eloquence) the story of a little vice-consul from Adrianople who couldn't make his first appointment with the consul because four orangutans were leashed in the consulate's antechamber. The vice-consul finally decides to go in but spends

---

7 Jean Revillon (1885–1963)—French furrier who, along with his English wife, Margaret, traveled to New York on the SS *Oregon*. Revillon Frères was the premier fur and luxury goods company in France. Jean was a manager for the New York City office with an apartment in the city. SS *Oregon* Passenger List.

8 Nadine Dahoui ("Mme. D")—Polish wife of Albert Dahoui, counselor at the French Embassy in New York and a French-Algerian like Camus. SS *Oregon* Passenger List.

his days at the consulate in fear. Finally, having been told by
the consul that one of the animals died after eating a box of
matches, the vice-consul brings a box every day and affectionately feeds it to one of the animals until it dies. When all the
beasts are dead and buried, then he breathes easy.

A classic story, as well, about 30-year-old consuls in Jeddah
and other such places who drink themselves to death in solitude (for me).

We're to pass the Azores in the evening, so I go on deck after dinner, and in a corner sheltered from the gusty wind that's
been blowing since we left, I enjoy a clear night, with a few
sparse but very large stars streaking above the ship, each with
the same rectilinear motion. In the sky, a sliver of moon casts
a dullish light that reflects evenly on the turbulent waters. I
gaze once again, as I have for years, at the drawings etched on
the surface by the foam and wake, that lace made and unmade,
that liquid marble … and once again I search for a comparison
exact enough to capture that marvelous blossoming of sea, of
water and light, a comparison that has for so long escaped me.
Still in vain. For me, it's a symbol that persists.

*

Friday. Saturday. Sunday. Same schedule. The sea still too
rough, we head south and pass the Azores. This microcosm
of society is at once fascinating and monotonous. Everyone
prides themselves on their elegance and savoir-vivre. Like seals
trained to do tricks. Some of them are opening up, though.
The Revillon furrier is on the boat. We learn he has a magnificent porcelain service, some superb silverware, etc., but that
he shows copies he's had made and keeps the originals locked
away. Likewise, it seems he also has a copy of a wife with whom
he's only ever made a copy of love.

Camus with friends, clowning on the deck of the SS
Oregon. © Collection Catherine et Jean Camus, Fonds
Albert Camus, Cité du Livre d'Aix-en-Provence.

Three or four passengers are obviously going to the U.S.A.
for the export of capital. I even let the scheme, quite crafty in
itself, be explained to me. "You'll notice," one of them says,
"that I'm not doing anything against the State. Its intentions
are good, but it doesn't understand anything about business."
These people here, they know about business. We agree with
R., always the charming companion, that the only contemporary problem is money. Unpleasant characters rotted by greed
and powerlessness. Thankfully, there's the company of women.
The truth and the light. Mme. D., more and more charming.
L., too.

*

Monday. Beautiful day. The wind has died down. For the first
time, the sea is calm. Passengers sprout up on deck like mush-
rooms after rain. We breathe easy. In the evening, a magnificent sunset. After dinner, moonlight on the sea. Mme. D. and
I agree most people don't lead the life they'd like to lead and
that this is a matter of cowardice.

*

Sunday. They announce we'll arrive in the evening. The week
passed in a whirlwind. Tuesday evening, the 21st, our table decides to celebrate the arrival of spring. Alcohol until 4 in the
morning. The next day, too. Forty-eight hours of pleasant euphoria, during which all our relationships quickly deepen. Mme. D.
is rebelling against her class. L. confesses to me the marriage
she's headed for is one of convenience. On Saturday, we exit
the Gulf Stream, and the temperature turns awfully chilly. Nevertheless, the time passes very quickly, and ultimately, I'm not
in such a rush to arrive. I've finished preparing my talk. In the
remaining time, I gaze out at the sea and chat, mostly with R.,
who's really quite smart—and with Mme. D. and L., of course.

At 12:00 in the afternoon, we catch sight of land. Seagulls
have been flying alongside the boat since morning, hanging
above the decks as if suspended and motionless. Coney Island, which looks like the Porte d'Orléans, is the first thing we
see. "It's Saint-Denis or Gennevilliers," L. says. It's absolutely
true. In the cold, with the gray wind and flat sky, it's all rather
gloomy. We'll anchor in the mouth of the Hudson but won't disembark until tomorrow morning. In the distance, Manhattan's
skyscrapers stand against a backdrop of mist. My heart is still
and cold, as it is when faced with sights that don't move me.

*

Monday. Went to bed very late last night. Got up very early. We sail through New York Harbor. A tremendous sight despite, or because of, the fog. Order, power, economic strength, they're all here. The heart trembles before so much remarkable inhumanity.

I don't disembark until 11 o'clock, after a long series of formalities where, out of all the passengers, I'm the one treated as suspect. The immigration officer ends up apologizing for having kept me. "I was required to do so, but I can't tell you why." A mystery—but after five years of occupation …

Welcomed by C., E., and an envoy from the consulate. C. hasn't changed. E. either.[9] With the whole circus over at immigration, the goodbyes with L., Mme. D., and R. are quick and cold.

Tired. My flu is coming back. I catch my first glimpse of New York on shaky legs. At first sight, a hideous, inhuman city. But I know people can change their mind. Here are the details that strike me: the garbage collectors wear gloves, the traffic is orderly, without the need for officers at the intersections,

9 Nicola Chiaromonte ("C.") (1905–72)—Italian writer, antifascist, veteran of the Spanish Civil War. He lived in Paris at the start of the war, fled France via Algeria, and stayed in Algiers in "The House above the World" portrayed in Camus's novel *A Happy Death*. Then he joined Camus in Oran, before finding passage to the US via Morocco. He reviewed *The Stranger* in the *New Republic*. See Albert Camus, Nicola Chiaromonte, *Correspondence, 1945–1962*, ed. Samantha Novello (Paris: Gallimard, 2019).

Pierre-André Emery ("E.") (1903–82)—Acquaintance from Camus's early days in Algeria, where they were both involved with the Théâtre du Travail. Emery lived in New York at the time of Camus's visit and was part of the welcoming party sent by Claude Lévi-Strauss.

A page from the writer's FBI file. Courtesy of the
United States Freedom of Information Act.

etc., no one ever has any change in this country, and everyone
looks as if they've just stepped off a low-budget film set. In the
evening, crossing Broadway in a taxi, tired and feverish, I'm
literally staggered by the circus of bright lights. I've come from
five years of night, and this intense and violent illumination

"Smoking" Camel cigarettes billboard in Times Square, 1943.
Photograph by John Vachon (1914–75). Library of Congress,
Prints & Photographs Division, Farm Security Administration/
Office of War Information Black-and-White Negatives.

is the first thing that gives me the impression of being on a
new continent (a huge 15 m. billboard advertising Camels: a
G.I., his mouth wide open, lets out huge puffs of *real* smoke.
All of it yellow and red). I go to bed as sick at heart as in body
but knowing perfectly well that I'll have changed my mind in
two days.

*

Tuesday. Get up with a fever. Unable to leave the room before
noon. When E. arrives, I'm a little better, and I go with him and
D., an adman originally from Hungary, for lunch at a French

restaurant. I notice that I haven't noticed the *sky-scrapers*,[10] that they've seemed only natural. It's a question of overall scale. And in any case, you can't always walk around with your head turned up. A person can keep only so many floors in sight at once. Magnificent food shops. Enough to make all of Europe burst. I admire the women in the streets, the hues of their dresses, and the color of the taxis, which look like insects dressed in their Sunday best, red and yellow and green. As for the tie shops, you have to see them to believe them. So much bad taste hardly seems imaginable. D. assures me Americans don't like ideas. That's what they say. I don't really trust "they."

At 3 o'clock, I go see Régine Junier.[11] Admirable spinster who sends me everything she can afford because her father died of tuberculosis when he was 27, and so ... She lives in two rooms, amid a mountain of homemade hats that are exceptionally ugly. But nothing could overshadow the generous and attentive heart that shines through in everything she says. I leave her, devoured by fever and unable to do anything but go back to bed. Too bad for the scheduled meetings. —New York's smell—a perfume of iron and cement—the iron dominates.

In the evening, dinner at Rubens[12] with L.M. He tells me the very "American Tragedy" story of his secretary. Married to a man with whom she's had two children, she and her mother come to find out the husband's a homosexual. Separation. The mother, a puritanical Protestant, works on the daughter for months, instilling the idea in her that her children are going to become degenerates. The idiot ends up suffocating one and

10 Here Camus has written *sky-scrapers* in English.
11 Régine Junier—French fashion designer living in New York who had corresponded with Camus and sent care packages of food and clothes to his family.
12 Most likely Reuben's Restaurant and Delicatessen on East 58th Street.

strangling the other. Declared not guilty by reason of insanity, she's set free. L.M. tells me his personal theory about Americans. It's the fifteenth one I've heard.

On the corner of East 1st Street, a small bistro where a screaming mechanical phonograph drowns out all conversation. To get five minutes of silence, you have to put in five cents.

*

Wednesday. A little better this morning. Liebling,[13] from the *New Yorker*, visits. Charming man. Chiaramonte then Rubé. These last two and I have lunch at a French restaurant. Ch. speaks of America as no one else does, in my opinion. I point out *Funeral Home* to him. He tells me how it works. One of the ways to understand a country is to know how people die there. Here, everything is planned. "*You die and we do the rest,*" the promotional flyers say.[14] Cemeteries are private property: "Hurry up and secure your spot." It's all bought and sold, the transport, the ceremony, etc. A dead man is a man who has lived a full life. —At Gilson's place, radio.[15] Then at my place with Ver-

13 A. J. Liebling (1904–63)—Reporter and essayist for the *New Yorker* who interviewed Camus at the Embassy Hotel. St Clair McKelway wrote up Liebling's interview notes for the "Talk of the Town" section of the magazine (see appendix A below). On Liebling and Camus, see Robert Zaretsky, "How A. J. Liebling became BFFs with Camus," *The Forward*, https://forward.com/culture/books/336672/how-aj-liebling-became-bffs-with-albert-camus/.

14 Both the words *Funeral Home* and the quotation are written in English in the original.

15 Paul Gilson (1904–63)—New York correspondent for French national radio broadcasting in 1945–46. After his return to France, he was in charge of arts programming on French national radio from 1946 to 1963. Unfortunately, no trace has survived of Camus's 1946 radio interview. [NB: he is not to be confused with the philosopher Etienne Gilson who was teaching in Toronto in the same period.]

cors, Thimerais, and O'Brien. We discuss tomorrow's talk.[16] At 6 o'clock, a drink with Gral at the Saint-Regis. I walk back to the hotel along Broadway, lost in the crowd and the enormous illuminated signs. Yes, there's an American tragedy. It's what's oppressed me since I arrived here, though I don't know what it's made of yet.

On Bowery Street, a street where the bridal shops stretch for more than 500 meters. I eat alone in the restaurant from this afternoon. And I come back to write.

The Negro Question. We sent a man from Martinique on assignment here. We put him up in Harlem. Vis-à-vis his French colleagues, he saw, for the first time, he wasn't of the same race.

An observation to the contrary: an average American sitting in front of me on the bus stood to give his seat to an older Negro lady.

Impression of overflowing wealth. Inflation is on the way, an American tells me.

16 Camus, Vercors, and Thimerais are planning the round table at Columbia University's McMillin Theater on March 26, 1946 with Justin O'Brien, the organizer.

Vercors (1902–91)—Pseudonym of Jean Bruller, a writer and illustrator and author of *Silence of the Sea*, a classic allegory of resistance, published underground in 1942 by the press he founded with Pierre de Lescure, Éditions de Minuit.

Thimerais (1900–1990)—Pseudonym of Léon Motchane, mathematician and the founder of the Institut des Hautes Études Scientifiques, whose *La Pensée patiente* (Patient Thought) was published in 1943 by Éditions de Minuit.

Justin O'Brien (1906–68)—Professor of French at Columbia. O'Brien translated *The Myth of Sisyphus*, *The Fall*, and *Exile and the Kingdom* and adapted *Caligula* for Broadway.

Camus's speech, "The Crisis of Man" (La Crise de l'homme), originally translated by Lionel Abel, is newly translated by Quintin Hoare in *Speaking Out: Lectures and Speeches, 1937–1958* (New York: Vintage, 2021).

Yank Reporter To Appear on CURC Station

Starting a new policy of bringing distinguished veterans to the Campus, the Columbia Show Shop, featured CURC program, announced today that Walter Bernstein, ex-Yank correspondent and first reporter to interview Marshal Tito, Yugoslav leader, will appear on this Thursday's program at eight-thirty. Listeners to the Campus radio station will hear Mr. Bernstein discuss his troubles with Army brass in reporting the news for Yank.

The Columbia Show Shop, featuring the singing of Fred Duhl the Columbia singer of folk songs, and Judy Dvorkin, the Barnard Balladeer, expects to continue with weekly guests secured through the cooperation of the Collegiate Post of The American Legion. On the list for the near future are Marion Hargrove, famous for potato peeling, and "See Here Private . . ."; Justin Gray, Yank Correspondent and first G.I. into Tokio.

Barnard Show

(Continued from page 2)
administration censors cut several digs at food and professors. Star of the Show, for our money, was Betsy Brigham who, as Jo Adams, led the cast in explaining last week's statement by our revered contemporary the "Barnard Bulletin" that "the girls . . . . will wear the usual Barnard clothes which will add greatly to the hilarity of the show."

Much of the music was borrowed from such varied sources as the "Atchinson, Topeka and Santa Fe," "I've Been Working on the Railroad," and Bob Hope's "Thanks for the Memory." Four original songs were written by Doris Johnson and Ann Lissfelt. Lyrics for these and the other songs were by Helen Trevor. Best were "It Must Be Something I Ate" a touching ballad about Columbia men and "We Ain't the Waldorf" a lament by the drugstore soda jerks.

All in all an amusing and entertaining show. You missed it? Well don't cry little man. Varsity Show tickets are now on sale in John Jay lobby. There's a show you cant' afford to miss.
F. M. K.

A Note on the Resistance, The Absurd. and M. Camus

The gentleman in the picture on the right is Albert Camus, who arrived yesterday from France and who will be one third of the discussion of "The Crisis of Man" at McMillin Theatre on Thursday night at 8:30.

M. Camus, who, with a group of friends, organized and published an underground newspaper named Combat, belongs to the group of French writers of the liberation, who, although fairly leftist, never approached the actual communistic tendencies of his league, Louis Aragon.

Camus, called by Professor Justin O'Brien in an article in the March 24 New York Tribune Book Review, the "Boldest Writer in France Today", has made considerable contribution to contemporary French letters not only as a journalist, but in the various fields of the novel, drama, and philosophy as well.

All of his thought is typified

ALBERT CAMUS

by an essays which he wrote in 1942, entitled "The Myth of Sisyphus", and which develops his premise that far too many intellectuals today recognise the absurdity of human life, and consequently see all occurrence as itself occurring on the same level of chance. Camus, however, prefers to live happily within this absurd, and not to sacrifice his lucidity and contentedness at the altar of metaphysical revelation of the true nature of the great absurdity.

Besides Camus, the symposium at McMillin will present Vercors, and Thimerais, two equally famous writers of the resistance.

CURC

TUESDAY, MARCH 26
8:30—Debate Council
9:00—French Program
9:20—The Whistler
9:45—Sports Parade
10:00—Columbia Campus Ballroom
10:30—The Symphonic Hour
WEDNESDAY, MARCH 27
8:00—Drama
8:15—Swedish program
8:30—Gems of Jazz
9:15—West End Jazz
9:45—Sports Parade
10:00—Sweet Swing
10:30—The Symphonic Hour
THURSDAY, MARCH 28
8:00—Music Box
8:15—Italian program
8:30—Show Shop
9:00—Jukes at St. Lukes
9:45—Sports Parade
10:00—It's All Yours
10:30—The Symphonic Hour

PNYX Organization Unites University's Greek Students

PNFX, the Geek organization, is one of the most active groups on the campus despite its small numbers. Found, on occasion, bunched together in one of the dark corners of Earl Hall they can be persuaded to tell their story.

In 1924, six or seven Greek Orthodox men, about 35 years old, who were still in college for some odd reason, decided to form a little group. Little did they realize that their social club would grow into the "Intercollegiate Federation of Hellenic Societies of New York".

Only 140 members are in this organization at Columbia but each one of them has an endless supply of energy in the rich Greekish red blood. Every other Friday from 7:30 to 10 P.M. they come darting on the campus from all parts of the university to meet in Earl Hall.

Another collection is being taken among the members in order to raise enough money to send Greek students to Columbia on free scholarships. The PNYXers are not altogether filthy with money so they are only raising money for one student, at the present time.

The club leader Peter Casmagios and his female assistant Nitsa Spanas are making plans for a dance to be held May 3 at John Jay. All Columbians will be invited to this social event and perhaps as a special treat some Greek Jazz will be played.

Trackmen Prepare For Bright Outdoor Season

Track coach Carl Merner continues to mold his men into top shape and keep them in condition in preparation for the initial outdoor meet at Philadelphia on April 26 and 27.

With the circular boards no longer on South Field, the team will move to Baker Field's dirt track as soon as it is usable, probably some time this week. In the meantime workouts are being held on South Field on an imaginary track.

After a fine showing in the A.A.U. meet two weeks ago, a steadily improving team is expected and C.U.'s chances in the Penn Relays in April look more optimistic than in the beginning of the season.

Columbia Spectator, announcing the "Crisis of Man" roundtable, Tuesday, March 26, 1946. Courtesy of the *Columbia Daily Spectator*.

*

Thursday. Spent the day dictating my talk. A few jitters in the evening, but I head straight out, and the audience is "glued." But then, while I'm speaking, someone filches the cashbox, the proceeds of which were to go to French children. At the end of the talk, O'Brien announces what's happened, and some-one in the audience stands up to suggest everyone give the same amount on the way out that they gave on the way in. On the way out, everyone gives much more and the proceeds are considerable. Typical of American generosity. Their hospitality and cordiality are also like this, immediate and without affectation. This is what's best about them.

*

Their fondness for animals. A multistory pet shop: canaries on the second floor, great apes at the top. A couple of years ago, a man was arrested on 5th Avenue for driving a giraffe around in his truck. He explained that his giraffe didn't get enough air out in the suburbs where he kept it and that he'd found this to be a good way to get it some air. In Central Park, a lady brought a gazelle to graze. To the court, she explained that the gazelle was a person. "Yet it doesn't speak," the judge said. "Oh, yes, it speaks the language of lovingkindness." Five-dollar fine. There's also the 3-kilometer tunnel under the Hudson and the impressive bridge to New Jersey.

After the talk, a drink with Schiffrin and Dolorès Vanetti— who speaks the purest slang I've ever heard—and with others, too.[17] Madame Schiffrin asks if I was ever an actor.

17 Jacques Schiffrin ("J.S.") (1892–1950)—Founder and director of Éditions de la Pléiade, the series of literary classics published by Gallimard. He was forced to leave France after being dismissed by the French publisher in the wake of anti-Semitic laws. Exiled to New York as of 1941, he founded Pan-

*

Friday. Knopf.[18] 11 o'clock. Cream of the crop. 12. Broadcasting. Gilson's a nice guy. We'll go see the Bowery together. I have lunch with Rubé and J. de Lannux, who drives us around New York afterward.[19] Beautiful blue sky that reminds me we're at the same latitude as Lisbon, which is hard to imagine. In tune with the flow of traffic, the gold-lit skyscrapers turn and spin in the blue above our heads. A moment of pleasure.

We go to Tryon Park above Harlem, where we tower over the Bronx on one side and the Hudson on the other. Magnolias blooming pretty much everywhere. I try a new type of these *ice-cream* that I enjoy so much.[20] Another moment of pleasure.

At 4 o'clock Bromley is waiting for me at the hotel. We're off to New Jersey. Immense landscape of factories, bridges, and railroads. Then, all of a sudden, East Orange, the most postcard-perfect countryside there could be, with thousands of

theon Books, which published a French language edition of *L'Étranger* in the US in 1946. See Amos Reichman, *Jacques Schiffrin: A Publisher in Exile, from Pléiade to Pantheon*, trans. Sandra Smith, foreword by Robert Paxton (New York: Columbia University Press, 2019).

Dolorès Vanetti Ehrenreich (1912–2008)—Radio journalist in New York in the 1940s. She produced a women's broadcast for the Voice of America at Pierre Lazareff's division of the Office of War Information and contributed a column to Vogue, "Europe for Beginners." Part of the vibrant social world of the wartime French exiles (Breton, Léger, Saint-Exupéry, Duchamp), she was a guide, and then a lover of Jean-Paul Sartre during his 1945 American tour. She served briefly as Camus's guide, as well.

18 Knopf—Camus could be referring to the publishing company ("big time") or to Alfred Knopf (1892–1984), the founder, or to his wife, cofounder Blanche Knopf (1894–1966). They published Camus's work in English.

19 Pierre de Lanux (1887–1955)—French writer and diplomat, married to American artist Eyre de Lanux.

20 *"Ice-cream"* is written in English in the original.

cottages, neat and tidy, set down like toys amid the tall poplars and magnolias. They take me to see the small public library, bright and cheery and used by the whole neighborhood—with its giant children's reading room. (Finally a country that really takes care of its children.) I look up philosophy in the card catalogue: W. James and that's it.[21]

At Bromley's, American hospitality (though his father is from Germany). We work on the translation of *Caligula*, which he's finished. He explains to me that I don't know how to handle my own publicity, that I have a "*standing*" I should be taking advantage of and that *Caligula*'s success here will allow me—my children and me—to be free from want. According to his calculations, I'll earn $1,500,000. I laugh, and he shakes his head. "Oh, you have no *sense*."[22] He's the best of fellows, and he wants us to go to Mexico together. (Nota: he's an American who doesn't drink!)

*

Saturday. Régine. I take over the gifts I brought for her, and she sheds tears of happiness.

A drink at Dolorès's, then Régine takes me to see some American department stores. I think of France. In the evening, dinner with L.M. From the top of the Plaza, I admire the island, covered in its stone monsters. At night, with its millions

21 Harald Bromley ("B.") (1909–76)—Aspiring producer who sought Camus's help on a translation of *Caligula* and dreamed of a production. He entertained Camus at his home in New Jersey and later drove Camus north to Quebec through the Adirondacks, in a secondhand car bought for the occasion. (In Montreal they learned that Camus's talk was canceled because of threats by supporters of Vichy France.)

William James (1842–1910)—Psychologist and philosopher associated with American pragmatism; brother of Henry James.

22 Both "standing" and "sense" are written in English in the original.

of illuminated windows and tall black building faces blinking
and flashing halfway up to heaven, it makes me think of a gi-
gantic blaze burning itself out, leaving thousands of immense,
black carcasses along the horizon, studded with smoldering
embers. The charming countess.

*

Sunday. A stroll to Staten Island with Chiaromonte and Abel.[23]
On the way back, in Lower Manhattan, immense geological ex-
cavations between tightly packed skyscrapers. As we walk past,
the feeling of something prehistoric overtakes us. We have dinner in China Town. For the first time, I'm able to breathe easy,
finding real life there, teeming and steady, just as I like it.

*

Monday morning. Stroll with Georgette Pope,[24] who came all
the way to my hotel, God knows why. She's from New Caledonia. "What is your husband's job?"
  "Magician!"[25]
From the top of the Empire State Building, in a glacial wind,
we admire New York, its ancient waters and flood of stone.

23 Nicola Chiaromonte ("C.")—See p. 27n9 above.
  Lionel Abel (1910–2001)—Art and literary critic and playwright closely
associated with *Partisan Review* and a member of the second generation of the
group known as "the New York Intellectuals." Abel translated Camus's speech
"The Crisis of Man" for Dorothy Norman's magazine, *Twice a Year*.
24 Georgette O'Connor Pope Day (1920–?)—Born in New Caledonia and
later naturalized American, she was performing a magic act with her husband,
Glen Kent Pope, when Camus met her. She also worked as a freelancer for
Paris-Presse and *France-Illustration*—and may have been seeking an interview
to place in France.
25 The question and response are written in English in the original manuscript.

At lunch, Saint-Ex's wife[26]—an exuberant person—tells us that back in San Salvador her father had had, alongside 17 legitimate children, forty bastards, each of whom received a hectare of land.

Evening, interview at the École libre des Hautes Études.[27] Tired, I go to Broadway with J.S.

Rolley Skating on W. 52nd Street.[28] A huge velodrome covered in red velvet and dust. In a rectangular box perched close beneath the ceiling, an old woman plays a most eclectic mix of tunes on a pipe organ. Hundreds of sailors, of girls dressed for the occasion in jumpsuits, pass from arm to arm in an infernal racket of metal wheels and pipe organ. This description could be pushed further.

Then Eddy et Léon, a charmless club.[29] To make up for it,

26 Consuelo de Saint-Exupéry (1901–79)—Widow of Antoine de Saint-Exupéry. Camus met with her as a representative from Gallimard, Saint-Exupéry's French publisher, which was suing Reynal & Hitchcock, Saint-Exupéry's American publisher, over rights to two of his books.

27 The École libre des Hautes Études (Free School of Advanced Studies) was founded by the Free French and Belgian governments-in-exile during World War II. Housed at the New School in New York City, it offered academic appointments to French scholars who had fled Europe, such as Jean Wahl and Claude Lévi-Strauss.

28 "Rolley Skating" is written in English in the original. Given the address and the date, this must have been Gay Blades, which in 1946, the year Camus visited, hosted the National Roller-Skating Championship. In 1956, the building became home to the famous Roseland Ballroom, which continued to operate until 2014. Camus's companion at the skating rink was Jacques Schoeller (1909–2002), referred to here both as JS and J, and not to be confused with the editor Jacques Schiffrin. Camus met Schoeller through Michel and Janine Gallimard. Schoeller, a journalist who had worked for Éditions Gallimard in magazine and advertising ventures, was a great connoisseur of New York night life (Lottman, *Albert Camus: A Biography*).

29 Leon and Eddie's, which Camus calls "Eddie et Léon," was a New York City nightclub that reached the height of its fame around World War II. It hosted

Leon and Eddie's nightclub, New York, 1945. © Andreas
Feininger/The LIFE Picture Collection/Shutterstock.

Camus and Jacques Schoeller on the town. © Collection Catherine et
Jean Camus, Fonds Albert Camus, Cité du Livre d'Aix-en-Provence.

J.S. and I have ourselves photographed as Adam and Eve, like
one of those photographs you find at fairs, where there are two
completely naked cardboard cutouts with openings at the head
where you can put your face through.

J., who has good things to say about American love, wants to
introduce me to some taxi girls. A small, dusty room with dim
lighting. Each ten-cent coin gives you the right to a dance. But
if you want to chat with the lady, you have to sit in the back

---

such notable performers as Bob Hope, Red Skelton, Jackie Gleason, and Harry
Belafonte.

of the room on either side of a small barrier and you're not allowed to get close. Feeling of repression and terrible sexual frustration. J. tells me about *V Day*[30] and the orgy-like scenes in Times Square.

*

Tuesday. With charming Harold, who also tells about American women. In the evening, the irritating French Institute. But then we go to a Negro nightclub with Dr. Jerry Winter. Rocco, the Negro pianist,[31] is the best I've heard in years. He plays standing in front of a rolling piano that he pushes in front of him. The rhythm, the force, the precision of his playing, the way he puts his whole self into it, jumping, dancing, throwing head and hair right and left.

*

Impression that only Negroes give life, passion, and nostalgia to this country that they colonize in their own way.

*

Night in the Bowery. The poverty—which gives a European the urge to say: "At last, reality." The real wreckage. The twenty-cent hotels. Bowery Follies where elderly singers perform for impoverished listeners in a space made up like a "saloon."[32] And then, only steps away, the most splendid bridal shops you could ever see—all lined up—windows sparkling, etc. Yes, an astonishing night.

---

30 In English in the original.
31 Maurice Rocco (1915–1976)—African-American singer, composer, pianist, and actor, famous for nightclub performances.
32 Sammy's Bowery Follies opened at 267 Bowery in 1934. Initially, it served as a dive bar for the down-and-out, but by the 1940s it began to attract more upscale clients who wanted to play at slumming it. The bar closed in 1969.

*

W. Frank. One of the few exceptional men I've met here. He despairs a little for today's America and compares it to that of the XIXth century. "The great minds (Melville) have always been solitary here."[33]

*

Vassar College. An army of young, long-legged starlets crossing on the lawns. What they do for young people here is worth remembering.

*

Sunday. Long conversation with Ch. Could we remake the church as a secular institution?

With students in the afternoon. They don't feel the real problem and yet their yearning is clear to see. In this country where *everything* is put toward proving life isn't tragic, they feel as if something is missing. This great effort is moving, but we have to reject the tragic *after* having looked it in the face, not before.

*

Monday. Ryder and Figari. Two truly great painters. Ryder's paintings, with their mystic inspiration and almost traditional technique (they're almost enamels), inevitably call Melville to mind, who was more or less his contemporary (younger). Yes,

33 Waldo Frank (1889–1967)—American journalist, novelist, and activist who wrote extensively about Latin American and Spanish literature; co-editor and contributor to *America and Alfred Stieglitz: A Collective Portrait* (1934).

Herman Melville's *Moby Dick* was an inspiration for Camus's turn to allegory in *The Plague* (1947), the novel he was working on during his North American travels.

America's greatness is there. And now? Figari has it all: yearning, strength, humor.[34]

Then Alfred Stieglitz, a sort of aged American Socrates.[35] "The older I get, the more and more beautiful life seems—but the more and more difficult it is to live. Don't expect anything from America. Are we an end or a beginning? I think we're an end. We're a country that doesn't understand love."

Evening. Circus. Three-ring. Everyone doing something at the same time—and I can't follow a thing.

Tucci:[36] How very easy human relationships are here because there are no human relationships here. They remain superficial. Out of respect and laziness.

Here in New York, thousands of would-be admirals and generals are doormen, captains, and boys. The elevator operators like so many bottled genies going up and down in their big boxes.

*

April 19. Another night in the Bowery. The *elevated*[37]—we're at the front—barrels along five stories up, and the skyscrapers slowly bend around us and the engine swallows the little red and blue lights and then stops to digest for a moment at one of the small stations and then resumes its course through poorer and poorer neighborhoods where fewer and fewer cars drive.

34 Albert Pinkham Ryder (1847–1917)—American painter inspired by Wagner and Shakespeare; known for moody and mystical seascapes.

Pedro Figari (1861–1938)—Uruguayan painter, close to Pierre Bonnard and Philippe Soupault.

35 Alfred Stieglitz (1864–1938)—Eminent American photographer who also ran galleries in New York that displayed avant-garde European art; husband of Georgia O'Keeffe.

36 Niccolò Tucci (1908–99)—Italian-American antifascist writer and friend of Nicola Chiaromonte.

37 In English in the original.

Sammy's nightclub on the Bowery, 1944. © Weegee (Arthur Fellig)/International Center of Photography/Getty Images.

Once again, the Bowery Follies and the old women who sing there at the end of their careers. Enormous, their makeup-caked faces oozing—suddenly starting to stamp their feet so that their rolls of blubbery flesh jiggle. "I'm a bird in a gilded cage."[38]

"Me? I've got no ambition."

"I'm nobody's baby," etc.

The least ugly are a flop. They have to be either *very beautiful* or *very ugly*. Instructive. There's mediocrity even in ugliness.

38 "A Bird in a Gilded Cage" was a popular parlor song in the early 1900s. The lyrics are given here as Camus noted them.

Then the night. Surrounded by squalor, a group of Romanians sing and dance until they're out of breath. Transported to the edge of an exalted land—and that unforgettable face.

*

When you look out from the heights of Riverside, the Highway, which runs along the Hudson, is an unbroken line of smooth-sailing, well-oiled cars letting loose a song both grave and distant, exactly like the sound of waves.

In Philadelphia, small cemeteries filled with flowers lie beneath enormous gas tanks.

*

Gentleness of evenings out on the vast lawns of Washington, the sky turning red and the grass beginning to darken, throngs of Black children playing there, hitting a ball with a wooden stick and crying out in joy as Americans in rumpled shirts sit slumped on benches—having come straight from a saloon like the kind you see in old movies—using their last bit of energy to suck on ice-creams molded into waxed-paper cups, while from under people's feet squirrels dig up treats only they know how to name and, in the hundred thousand trees of this city, against a still-light sky, a million birds salute the appearance of the first star above the Washington obelisk, while long-legged creatures stride along the grass paths, the grand monuments behind them, and, in a moment of relaxation, offer their splendid faces to the sky, their loveless gazes.

*

Plague: it's a world without women and so a stifling one.

*

The one who is right is the one who has never killed. So then it can't be God.

*

My curiosity about this country has suddenly ended. As with certain people whom I turn away from without being able to explain why and without being able to maintain interest (F.[39] reproaches me for this). Though I can see the thousands of reasons someone would have for being interested in this place, and I could defend and advocate for it, could reconstruct its beauty or its future prospects, still my heart has simply stopped speaking and ...

*

Chinese theater in China Town. A large hall, dusty and round. The show runs from 6:00 to 11:00 P.M. and takes place in front of 1,500 Chinese people, who eat peanuts, chatter, enter, exit, and follow the show with a sort of constant distraction. Children run around in the middle of the hall. Onstage, costumed actors perform alongside musicians in business suits and suspenders, who break off from time to time to have a sandwich or pull up a child's pants. Similarly, throughout the performance, stagehands in vests and shirtsleeves come and go, collecting a sword fallen from the hand of a dead man, setting a chair in place or removing one, all of it done for no particular reason. From time to time, actors waiting to make their entrance can be seen standing in the doorways that lead backstage, chatting or following the action.

As for the play itself, given the show is in Chinese, I try to conjure up the storyline. I suspect I've only misinterpreted things, though, for just as a brave man is dying onstage in

39 Camus's wife, Francine Faure Camus (1914–1979).

a most realistic fashion, his wife and friends wailing around him, at that very moment, right when everything seems very serious, the audience laughs. Then, at the clownish entrance of a sort of foghorn-voiced magistrate, I'm the only one who laughs while the rest of the audience shows a sort of respectful attention. A sort of butcher covered in blood kills a man. He forces a Chinese boy to carry the body. The Chinese boy is so scared his knees knock together ...

*

From New York to Canada

*

Clean, wide-open countryside with houses small and large, the latter with white columns and tall, sturdy trees, with lawns that are never separated by fences, so that a single lawn belongs to everyone, a lawn where beautiful children and lithe adolescents laugh before a life filled with the good things, with rich crèmes. Here, nature contributes to those beautiful American fairy tales.

*

A narrative about an American childhood in which the child searches in vain for his heart's calling. He gives up.

*

The owl who was playing the drums at the Bowery Follies.

*

Two people are in love with each other, but don't speak the same language. One speaks both languages but speaks the one they share imperfectly. For them, being able to love each other is enough. The one who knows both languages dies. Her last words are in her native tongue, which the other is helpless to grasp. He's trying to figure it out, trying to figure it out ...

*

Small inn in the heart of the Adirondacks, a thousand miles from civilization. Upon entering the bedroom, a strange feeling: a man arrives, on a business trip, with no preconceived notions, in the wilderness, in a remote inn. There, amid nature's silence, amid the room's simplicity, amid the remoteness from civilization, he decides to stay for good, to cut all ties with what his life was and never again let anyone know he's alive.

*

New England and Maine. Lands of lakes and red houses. Montreal and the two hills. A Sunday. Boredom. Boredom. The only amusing thing: the trams that look, in their shape and gilding, like carnival rides. This great country, calm and slow. You get the feeling it's completely unaware of the war. Europe, which was centuries ahead in knowledge, has just, in a few short years, gained several centuries in awareness.

*

Remake and recreate Greek thinking as a rebellion against the sacred, but not a rebellion against the Romantic sacred— itself a form of the sacred—but a rebellion that puts the sacred in its place.

The idea of messianism is at the root of all fanaticism. Messianism in exchange for man. Greek thinking is not historical. The values are *preexistent. Against modern* existentialism.[40]

40 In other words, against Sartre's famous "existence precedes essence" proposition. In Camus's journals, interviews, and letters, he continually expresses frustration at being linked with existentialism, a philosophy he impugned in *The Rebel*.

*

Plague. Tarrou[41] spends most of his time with Spanish dancers. He loves only passion. Naturally, a man has to fight. "But if he's stopped loving other things, then what's the point of fighting?"

*

In the American newspapers: a weapon more terrible than the atomic bomb, "the Black Plague killed 60% of the population in some places during the Middle Ages. We don't know if American scientists have found ways to spread it, but the Japanese were unable to do so in China, where they'd sown the black plague in rice."

*

Québec's spectacular landscape. At the tip of Cap Diamant, facing the immense opening of the Saint Lawrence, air, light, and water come together in an infinite expanse. For the first time while on this continent, the real impression of beauty and true greatness. It seems I should have something to say about Québec, about its past, about men coming here to struggle in solitude, driven by a force greater than themselves. But what's the point? I know now there are many things, artistically speaking, I could *accomplish*. But this word no longer holds any meaning for me. The only thing I'd like to say I've so far been unable to say and I'll probably never be able to say.

*

Do a play about bureaucracy (as stupid in America as elsewhere).

41 Tarrou—Beloved character in Camus's *The Plague* who keeps poetic notebooks about absurd people he observes in Oran.

*

Even the Salvation Army advertises here. And in their advertisements, Army women have rosy cheeks and glittering smiles ...

*

Zaharo's father.[42] Polish. At fifteen, slaps an officer. Runs away. Arrives in Paris during Carnival. Buys confetti with the few sous he has and resells it. Thirty years later, he has a huge fortune and a family. Completely illiterate. His son reads him things at random. Reads him the Apology of Socrates. "You don't have to read me any other books," the father says. "This one says it all." He's been having the same book read to him ever since. He hates judges and police.

*

Manhattan. Above the *sky-scrapers*, through hundreds of thousands of high walls, a tugboat cry sometimes turns up in the midst of your insomniac night, reminding you this desert of iron and cement is an island.

*

The guy in the Holland Tunnel in New York or the Sumner Tunnel in Boston. All day long on an elevated walkway, counting the cars that endlessly pass in a deafening racket, the length of the tunnel violently lit and too long for him to see any exit. A hero made for the modern novel.

42 Leon Zaharo (1898–?)—Paris-born furrier who lent Camus his apartment in the Century building at 25 Central Park West, after the writer left the Embassy Hotel.

*

B. as a superior American. His psychology: mariners love the mountains, and mountaineers love the sea.

*

Rain over New York. It continuously falls between tall cubes of cement. Odd feeling of estrangement in the taxi, its quick, monotonous windshield wipers sweeping away waters endlessly reborn. Impression that I'm trapped in this city, that I could escape the blocks immediately surrounding me and run for hours without finding anything other than new cement prisons, without the hope of a hill, a real tree, or a face overcome with emotion.

*

B.'s father. Supreme Court judge in Hamburg. His bedside reading is the German Indicateur Chaix, which lists the arrivals and departures of all the world's trains.[43] He knows it practically by heart, and B. notes this oddity with an admiration completely devoid of irony.

*

Rains of New York. Incessant, sweeping over everything. The skyscrapers rise above the gray haze like the immense, whitish sepulchers of this city of the dead. Through the rain, you can see the sepulchers swaying on their foundations.

Terrible feeling of abandonment. Even if I were to hold everyone in the world tight against me, I still wouldn't be protected from anything.

---

43 Camus would give this bit of backstory to Tarrou's father in *The Plague*.

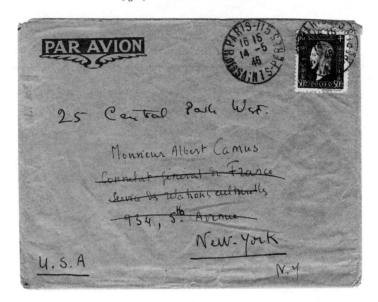

Mail forwarded to Central Park West. © Collection Catherine et Jean
Camus, Fonds Albert Camus, Cité du Livre d'Aix-en-Provence.

*

Plague. To Tarrou: "So then, you believe you know all there is
to know about life?"
Tarrou: "Yes."

*

Rebel. In-depth analysis of the Terror and its relationship with
bureaucracy.
—Note that our age marks the end of ideologies. The
atomic bomb prohibits ideology.[44]

---

44 This idea recurs throughout a series of articles Camus published in the Resistance newspaper *Combat*. Each article was printed with its own individual
title, under the overall title "Neither Victims nor Executioners."

*

Julien Green wonders (*Journal*) if it's possible to imagine a saint writing a novel.[45] Of course not, because there can be no novel without rebellion. Or we'd have to imagine a novel that indicts the earthly world and man—a novel completely devoid of love. Impossible.

*

At sea[46]

*

The longueur of this return trip. Evenings at sea and the passage from sunset to moonrise are the only times I feel my heart relax a little. I always have and always will love the sea. It always has and always will soothe all the things inside of me.

Terrible mediocrity of this environment. Until now, I've never once suffered from the mediocrity surrounding me. Until now. But here this intimacy goes too far. At the same time, in all of them there's something that could go far, if only ...

Two young and beautiful people began a fling aboard the ship, and as soon as they did, a sort of nasty circle closed in on them. These beginnings of love! I love and approve of them from the bottom of my heart—with a form of gratitude, even,

45 Julien Green (1900–1998)—Catholic essayist, born in the United States, who wrote primarily in French. Known for his novels and for a nineteen-volume diary that explored his Catholic faith and his homosexuality with exceptional frankness. Elected to the French Academy in 1971.

46 Camus sailed from New York back to Le Havre on the cargo ship *Fort-Royal*, June 10–23. In May, he had sent back via the French Consulate a care package for his wife and children, including six pounds of sugar, six pounds of coffee, three pounds of powdered eggs, six pounds of flour, four pounds of rice, six pounds of chocolate, thirty pounds of baby food, twenty-eight pounds of soap, and an assortment of other items. See p. 54.

CONSULAT GENERAL DE FRANCE
A NEW YORK

DETAIL
----

d'une caisse contenant des vivres rationnés en France et du savon.

1.-Nom du voyageur:..... *C A M U S*   *Albert*

2.-Nom,prénoms, adresse complète des personnes auxquelles la caisse
est destinée:

Mme. *Albert* CAMUS ... *4 rue de l'université - Paris (7)*

... *France* ....

. . . .

3.-Degré de parenté avec le voyageur:.... *Épouse* ....

Nature des marchandises	Poids	Nature des marchandises	Poids
Sucre	*3* Kgs		Kg
Café	*3*		
Oeufs en poudre	*1,5*		
Pâtes FARINES	*3*		
RIZ	*2*		
Chocolat	*3*	*Poids du contenant :*	*25 à 30 kgs*
Vivres pour bébés	*15*		
Conserves viandes	*5*		
Conserves diverses	*5*		
Savons et lessives	*14*		

Poids total:............. *80* Kgs

CERTIFIE SINCERE -

New-York, le *21 Mai* -1946

Signature du Voyageur:

Albert Camus

List of rationed goods addressed to Mme Albert Camus in May 1946
via the French Consulate in New York. © Collection Catherine et Jean
Camus, Fonds Albert Camus, Cité du Livre d'Aix-en-Provence.

for those who, on this deck, in the middle of this Atlantic bursting with sun, midway between continents gone mad, sustain the truths of youth and love. So why not give a name to this longing that I, too, feel in my heart, to this tumultuous desire that leads me back to the restless heart I had at 20? But I know the remedy: I'll gaze out at the sea for a while.

Sad to still feel so vulnerable. In 25 years, I'll be 57. 25 years, then, to do my work and find what I'm looking for. Then, old age and death. I know what's most important to me. And I still find a way of giving in to those little temptations, of wasting time on pointless conversations or fruitless dawdling. I've mastered two or three things in myself. But how far I am from that excellence I'll need so much.

Wonderful night on the Atlantic. The hour between the sun disappearing and the moon barely emerging, between the still-luminous west and the already-dark east. Yes, I've truly loved the sea—that peaceful immensity—those wakes covered over—those liquid roads. For the first time, a horizon equal to human breath, a space as great as its audacity. I've always been torn between my appetite for people, the vanity of restlessness, and the desire to make myself measure up to those seas of forgetfulness, to those immeasurable silences that are like death's enchantment. I have a taste for the world's vanities, for my fellow man, for faces, but unlike this century, I have a rule I live by, which is the sea and everything in this world that resembles it. O sweet night, when all the stars spin and streak above the masts, and this silence in me, this silence at last delivers me from everything.

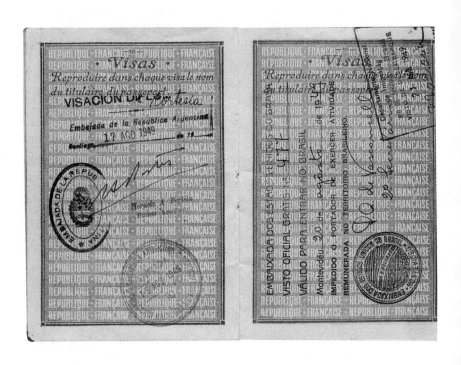

Visa stamps for Argentina and Brazil in Camus's
passport. © Collection Catherine et Jean Camus, Fonds
Albert Camus, Cité du Livre d'Aix-en-Provence.

Travels in
South America

June–August 1949

June 30

At sea. Exhausting day. R.[1] and I drive as fast as possible to make it to Marseille on time. Desdemona gets the job done. In Marseille, scorching heat and a wind strong enough to carve your face. Even nature is an enemy. Single room. I walk through the corridors and decks while waiting for departure. Feeling of shame on seeing the passengers in 4th class, housed in steerage, in berths stacked on top of each other, like in a concentration camp. Dirty diapers hung out to dry. Children are going to live in this hell for 20 days, and I ... The boat weighs anchor two hours late. Dinner. At my table, G., a history of philosophy professor at the Sorbonne—a short young man who's going to see his family in Argentina—and Mme. C., who's going to see her husband. She's from Marseille, a long, brunette girl. She says whatever pops in her head—and sometimes it's entertaining. Other times ... In any case, she's alive. The others are dead—and so am I, after all. After dinner, G., who's made some allusions to having experienced the plague, introduces me to a Brazilian professor and his wife as "the author of *The Plague*."

1 Robert Jaussaud ("R.")—Lifelong friend of Camus from Algeria; they met in one of Jean Grenier's philosophy classes and worked together in the 1930s in the Théâtre du Travail and the Théâtre de l'Équipe.
  Desdemona was Camus's nickname for his car, a black Citroën 11 CV.

I must look *really* good! In the "music hall" (where half the emigrants currently in 4th class could be comfortably housed), G.
plays us some trivial little snippets on the ship's piano, which
seems to have blown all its gaskets. Conversation follows. The
Brazilian professor praises Salazar. Mme. C. makes two huge
blunders in trying to convince the Brazilians that a revolu-
tion's happening every day in South America. I hear, "She's low
class, the lowest of the low," and other such pearls. I say goodbye and go on my way. In the rear of the boat, where I go to
take refuge, some emigrants are drinking wine from a wineskin
and singing. I stay with them, unknown and happy (for ten
seconds). Then I go gaze out at the sea. A crescent moon rises
above the masts. As far as the eye can see, in a still-clear night,
the sea—and a feeling of calm, a powerful melancholy, rises
from the waters then. I've always been able to make peace with
things out at sea, and for a moment the infinite solitude does
me good, though I can't help but feel all the world's tears are
rolling atop the sea now. I return to my cabin to write this—as
I'd like to do every evening, without getting into personal details, but forgetting none of the day's events. With an anxious
heart, my thoughts turn back to what I've left behind, and yet,
still, I'd like to get some sleep.

*

July 1

Waking with a fever, I stay in bed, dreaming and dozing for
part of the morning. At 11:00, I feel better and go out. G. on
deck. We talk philosophy. He wants to do a philosophy of the
history of philosophy. He's quite right. But, according to him,
he's young at heart and likes to live. Right again. Lunch with
my three musketeers. Mme. C. makes another blunder, asking
G. if he's a middle-school teacher, when really he teaches at the

Sorbonne. But she doesn't realize her mistake. I note the way men act with her. They think she's flighty because she's cheery. A mistake, of course. In the afternoon, I read an account of the Brazilian revolutions—Europe's got nothing on them. At five o'clock, I go work in the sun. The sun beats down on the sea, which is barely able to breathe, and the boat is weighed down with silent people from fore to aft. Unlike the people, the ship's record player screams its tunes out in every direction. I'm introduced to a young Romanian who's leaving England to go live in Argentina. A passionate woman—neither beautiful nor ugly, with a hint of a mustache. Then I go to my cabin to read, then get dressed again for dinner. Sad. I drink some wine. After dinner, conversation, but I'm gazing out at sea, trying once again to fix that image I've been seeking for twenty years, the patterns and drawings etched on the sea by waters cast aside by the bow. When I find it, it'll all be over.

Twice, the thought of suicide. The second time, still gazing at the sea, a frightful burning rises in my temples. Now I think I understand *how* a person kills himself. Return to the conversation—jaw-dropping. After having made some decisions about work, I climb, in the dark, to the upper deck and finish my day out in front of the sea, the moon, and stars. —The surface of the water is barely illuminated, but you can feel the depths of its darkness. That's how the sea is, and that's why I love it! The call of life and an invitation to death.

*

July 2

Monotony has set in. A little work in the morning. Sun on the upper deck. Before lunch, I end up being introduced to all the passengers. We're not spoiled with pretty women, but I say that without bitterness. All afternoon in view of Gibraltar, the sea suddenly calmed by that enormous rock of sloping cement, its face hostile and abstract. These are the trappings of power. Then Tangiers, with its comfortable white houses. At six o'clock, as the day comes to an end, the sea rises a little, and the ship's speakers boom the *Eroica*[2] as we pull away from the high, forbidding banks of Spain and leave Europe for good. My eyes never leave that land, my heart heavy.

After dinner, a movie. A high-octane American dud, of which I can only swallow the first few images. I go back to the sea.

*

July 3

The days all blend together. This morning, a dip in the pool (the water comes up to my stomach) and some ping-pong to finally stretch the muscles. This afternoon, horse racing (dice game) with my usual bad luck. We're on the Atlantic, and the boat's rolling a lot due to some large swells. Tried to work, but without much success. In the end, I read de Vigny's Journal, a lot of which is delightful, except that part of him that's like a constipated swan.[3] To all of that I prefer this clean and narrow cabin, this hard berth, and this destitution. Either this solitude without the superfluous or the storm of love, no, nothing else in the world interests me. Have I forgotten anything? I don't think so. I finish the day, as usual, in front of the sea, sumptuous this

2 Beethoven's Symphony no. 3, also known in Italian as *Sinfonia Eroica* (*Heroic Symphony*).

3 Alfred de Vigny (1797–1863)—French poet, novelist, dramatist, and translator. The work referred to here is his *Journal d'un poète* (*A Poet's Journal*). Alfred de Musset (1810–57) may be responsible for the swan image. In 1834, Musset drew a caricature of Vigny as "an old, constipated swan about to birth a proverb after a painstaking effort." https://art.rmngp.fr/en/library/artworks /alfred-de-musset_alfred-de-vigny_dessin-au-crayon_1834.

evening, beneath a moon that writes Arabic characters in phos-
phorescent lines atop the slow-moving swells. The sky and water are never-ending. What good company sadness finds there!

*

July 4[4]

Same sort of day. Aggravated by lethargy—as if the endless series of insomnia-filled nights has suddenly come calling. I lie
down several times during the day and drift off each time even
though I had a pretty good night. Other than that, work, pool,
sun (at 2 o'clock, since the rest of the time it's like a frog pond),
and de Vigny. A lot of what's written speaks to my current state
of mind. This, again: "If suicide is permissible, it's in one of
those situations where a man is too much in his family's way
and where his death would bring peace to all those whom his
life troubles." I should say, however, that tanned, rested, with a
full stomach, and dressed in light-colored clothes, I have all the
air of life in me. I could please someone, it seems—but whom?
 Facing the sea, before going to bed. This time the moon illuminates an entire corridor of sea that, with the ship's movement, seems, on the dark ocean, like a full and milky river
flowing tirelessly toward us. I'd already tried, during the day, to
make some notes about the sea, which I'll return to now:
 Morning sea: Enormous fishpond—heavy and wriggling—
scaly—sticky—covered in fresh slime.
 Afternoon sea: pale—a wide, white-hot sheet of metal—
sizzling, too—it'll flip over to offer its wet face, now in the
shadows, to the sun ... etc.
 Goodnight.

---

4 Like several of the entries Camus made on the trip to South America, parts
of this one would be incorporated into his essay "The Sea Close By."

*

July 5

Morning swim, then sun, then to work. At noon, we pass the Tropic of Cancer, beneath a vertical sun that kills all shadows. Still, it's not overly hot. The sky is filled with a bad fog, though, and the sun looks like a sickness. The sea looks like a great swell, with the metallic radiance of decomposition. In the afternoon, the big event: we pass an ocean liner traveling the same route as us. The salute the two boats give each other—three great cries from some prehistoric animal—the waving of passengers lost at sea, awakened by the presence of other people, and the final separation of those green, malevolent waters—all of this is a little heartrending. Afterward, I stay facing the water for a long time, full of a strange and good exhilaration. After dinner, I head to the fore. The emigrants are playing accordion and dancing in the night, and already the heat seems to be rising.

*

July 6

The day dawns on a steel sea, choppy and covered in blinding scales. The sky is white with fog and heat, with a dull but unbearable brightness, as if the sun had liquified and spread through the thick layers of cloud, over the entire expanse of the heavenly crown. As the day progresses, the heat climbs in the pallid air. All through the day, the bow flushes clouds of flying fish from their wavy bushes. At 7 P.M., the coast comes into view, gray and leprous. At night, we disembark in Dakar. Two or three cafés violently lit with neon, tall Black men admirable in dignity and elegance in their long white boubous,

Black women in traditional, brightly colored dresses, the scent of peanuts and dung, dust and heat. Only a couple of hours, but enough to pick up the scent of my Africa, the scent of poverty and dereliction, a virgin yet strong scent whose seduction I know. When I return to the boat, a letter. For the first time, I go to bed somewhat calmed.

*

July 7

Night of insomnia. Heat. Pool and then I go to stretch out in my cabin. I finish Vigny. After lunch, I try to sleep, in vain. I work until 6 P.M., with good results. Then I'm out on the promenade deck with this strange character I've been seeing since we first set out. Always dressed, even at the Tropic, in a suit of gray-black wool, stiff collar, traveling cap, black footwear, 60 years old. Short, thin, the look of a headstrong rat. Alone at a table, his deckchair always in the same place on the promenade deck, he reads nothing but *Les Nouvelles littéraires*, of which he seems to have an inexhaustible supply and which he reads from the first line to the last. He smokes cigar after cigar and doesn't talk to anyone. The only conversation I've heard him engage in was to ask a sailor if porpoises are fat or thin. He also sometimes has a drink (pastis) with a young Swiss-German man who doesn't speak French. He himself doesn't speak German. It makes for a conversation of deaf-mutes. This evening, following him four laps around the promenade deck, I noticed he didn't look at the sea a single time. Nobody onboard knows what he does for a living.

Before dinner, I watch the sun set. It's absorbed by the fog long before it reaches the horizon. At that moment, the sea is pink on the port side, blue on the starboard. We set out over a boundless expanse. There'll be no land until Rio. The evening hour grows suddenly wonderful. The water thickens, tarnishes a little. The sky stretches itself thin. At this hour of such great peacefulness, hundreds of porpoises rise from the water, prance and turnabout for a moment, and then flee toward a horizon without man. When they've left, the silence and anguish of primitive seas. After dinner, I return to the front of the boat, facing the sea. It's sumptuous, heavy, and embroidered. The wind whips my face with brutal force, coming at me head-on, having crossed stretches of space whose immensity I can't even imagine. I feel alone and a little lost, but ultimately enraptured, feeling my strength reborn little by little before this unknown future, this greatness that I love.

*

July 8

Night of insomnia. The whole day, I walk around with a hollow head and an empty heart. The sea is rough. The sky overcast. The decks are deserted. In fact, since Dakar, there are only about twenty passengers left. Too tired to describe the sea today.

*

July 9

Better night. In the morning, I walk on the large, empty decks. The trade winds we're encountering now have cooled things off. A clipped, heavy wind vigorously brushes the sea, which rolls back in small, foamless waves.

A little work, a lot of dawdling. I realize I haven't been writing down conversations with other passengers. Some of them are interesting, like the one with the publisher Delamain and his wife.[5] Read a charming novel by him about fidelity. I'll come back to it. Also because my current interest isn't really in people but in the sea and this profound sadness in me that I'm not used to.

At 6 P.M., at sunset, recordings of the great works are played, as they are every evening. Suddenly, *Toccata*,[6] just as the sun disappears behind the clouds accumulated along the horizon line. In this operatic sky, immense streaks of red gather with black stuffed animals, with fragile structures that seem to be made of wire and feathers, in a vast arrangement of red, green, and black—covering the entire sky, evolving with the oft-changing light, in step with the most majestic choreography. *Toccata*, over this sleeping sea, under this royal sky's celebrations ... the moment is unforgettable. So much so that the whole ship goes silent, the passengers pressed onto the decks, along the western edge, brought back to silence and what is truest in them, lifted for an instant from the misery of days and the pain of being.

*

July 10

We cross the equator in the morning, the weather as in the Seine-et-Oise[7]—brisk, a little cutting, the sky filled with sheep, the sea a little prickly. The ceremony in honor of crossing the

5 Maurice Delamain (1883–1974)—One of two directors of French publisher Éditions Stock. Delamain's *Double Ascension: une aventure de la fidelité* was published by Stock in 1945.

6 Most likely J. S. Bach's Toccata and Fugue in D Minor, BWV 565.

7 From 1790 through 1968, the Seine-et-Oise was a *département* (administrative division) of France covering, roughly, the western half of Paris, with Versailles as its *préfecture* (capital).

equator having been canceled, for lack of passengers, we replace those rites with some games in the pool. Then, a moment
with the emigrants playing the accordion and singing at the
front of the ship, facing toward the deserted sea. I again notice
a woman with them, already graying but high class, a beautiful
face, proud and gentle, hands and wrists like stems, and a look
like no other. Always followed by her husband, a tall, taciturn
blond man. Information gleaned: she's fleeing Poland and the
Russians and is taking exile in South America. She's poor. But,
looking at her, I think of those well-dressed maritornes[8] occu-
pying a couple of the first-class cabins. I haven't dared speak
to her yet.

A calm day. Aside from the grand champagne dinner in celebration of our having crossed the equator. Social gatherings
of more than four people are hard for me to bear. A story from
Mme. C: Her grandmother: "Oh, me? Well, in my life, you see,
I've only skimmed the surface of things." Her grandfather: "Go
on, my love, don't forget you've given me two sons!"

After dinner, the passengers are treated to some Laurel and
Hardy, but I dash off to the bow to contemplate the moon and
the Southern Cross toward which we're endlessly sailing. Surprised by how few stars there are in this southern sky and how
practically anemic they look. I think of our swarming Algerian
nights.

Remained in front of the sea for a long time. Despite all my
efforts and reasoning, impossible to shake this sadness that I
no longer even understand.

*

8 The term originates with Maritornes, a character in *Don Quixote*. In chap-
ter 16, Maritornes, a hunchbacked, half-blind servant at an inn where Quixote
and Sancho are staying, is, in the dark of night, confused with the innkeeper's
beautiful daughter and thus welcomed into Don Quixote's bed.

July 11

In the middle of the Intertropical Convergence Zone,[9] the day dawns beneath a battering rain. Buckets of water wash over the decks, but the temperature remains stifling and dead. In the middle of the day, the sky clears, but the sea is rough, and the ship pitches and rolls. Some defections from the dining room. Worked. Poorly. Toward the evening, little by little, the sky again fills with clouds, growing more overcast by the minute. Night falls fast over a sea of black ink.

*

July 12

Rain, wind, furious sea. People are sick. The ship sails forward, surrounded by a sea-spray smoke. Slept and worked. Toward the end of the afternoon, the sun makes its appearance. We're already at the latitude of Pernambuco[10] and are heading toward the coast. In the evening, the sky again grows overcast. Dramatic clouds come to greet us from the continent— messengers from a frightening land. That's the thought that suddenly comes to me and reawakens the absurd premonition I had before the trip. But the sun will dispel all of that.

*

July 13

A radiant sun endlessly floods the surface of the sea. The whole boat is bathed in a dazzling light. Pool, sun. I work all afternoon. The evening is cool and gentle. We arrive in two days.

9 The Intertropical Convergence Zone is more commonly referred to as "the doldrums," in reference to the lack of wind.

10 Pernambuco, a state in northeast Brazil, is just south of the Equator.

All of a sudden, the thought of leaving the boat, this narrow cabin where, during these long days, I've been able to shelter a heart turned away from everything, the thought of leaving this sea that's helped me so much, it frightens me a little. Beginning to live again, to speak. People, faces, a role to play, it'll require more courage than I feel. Fortunately, I'm in good shape, physically. But there are times when I'd like to avoid the human face.

Late at night, on a boat fast asleep, I gaze out at the night. The curious southern moon, pressed flat at the top, illuminates the waters to the south. You can imagine those thousands of kilometers, those solitudes where the thick, shiny waters are like an oily glebe. That, at least, would be peace.

*

July 14

Perpetual good weather. I finish up my work, or at least the work I've been able to carry out on the boat, having given up on the rest. In the afternoon, a few hundred meters out in the water, an enormous black beast rises to the surface, rolls atop a couple of waves, and sprays two jets of mist into the air. The busboy next to me claims it's a whale. Probably, given the size, the awesome force of its stroke, the solitary air surrounding the beast … but I remain skeptical. In the afternoon, mail and suitcases. In the evening, the captain's reception and the 14th of July dinner.[11] For the first time, sunset without fog. Brazil's first foothills, black and silhouetted, surround the sun, right and left. We dance, sign menus, exchange cards, and we all promise to see each other again, we give our word. Tomorrow, everyone will have forgotten everyone else. I go to bed late,

11 July 14 is Bastille Day, France's national day of celebration.

tired and telling myself to approach this country in a more relaxed state of mind.

*

July 15

At four in the morning, a commotion on the upper deck wakes
me. I leave my cabin. It's still dark out. The coast is very close,
though: a continuous line of rolling black hills, sharply silhouetted, yet the silhouettes are rounded, too—the aged edges of
one of the oldest lands on Earth. In the distance, some lights.
We follow along the coast as the night begins to lift, the water
barely rippling, and we tack, the lights in front of us now, but
still far away. I return to my cabin. When I go up again, we're
already in the bay, immense and steaming as the day breaks,
the light suddenly condensing into islands. The fog quickly
dissipates. We can see the lights of Rio running along the coast,
the "Sugarloaf," four lights on its summit and, on the highest of
the mountain's summits, which seems to lord over the city, an
immense and regrettable Christ stands illuminated. As the day
breaks, we can see the city better, huddled between the sea and
mountains, stretched out lengthwise, spreading out endlessly.
In the center, huge buildings. Every other minute, a rumbling
sounds above us: an airplane taking off in the dawning day,
blending in with the land at first, then rising up in our direction and passing over our heads with a great clamor of elytra.
We're in the center of the harbor, and the mountains form an
almost perfect circle around us. Eventually, a blood-red light
arrives, announcing the rising sun, which emerges from behind
the eastern mountains, facing the city, and begins to climb into
the pale, cool sky. The richness, the sumptuousness of the colors that then play on the harbor, the mountains, and the sky
cause everyone to fall silent once more. A minute later, the col-

ors are about the same, but it's a postcard now. Nature abhors miracles that go on too long.

Formalities. Then disembarkation. Instantly, it's the whirlwind I'd feared. Some journalists had already come aboard. Questions, photos. No better or worse than anywhere else. As soon as I reach Rio, though, where I'm welcomed by Mme. M.[12] and a great Brazilian journalist—already met in Paris, very nice—the real ordeal begins. Amid the confusions of this first day, a couple of random notes:

1°. They ask me to choose between a room at the embassy, which is deserted, and a room at one of the luxury hotels, which are everywhere. I run from the luxury hotel's ugly facade and am grateful to find one of the most basic, most charming rooms in a completely empty embassy.

2°. Brazilian drivers are either pleasure-seeking lunatics or cold sadists. The chaos and anarchy of the traffic know only one law: get there first, no matter the cost.

3°. A most striking contrast is displayed between the luxuriousness of the hotels and modern buildings and, sometimes only a hundred meters from the luxurious, the favelas, a sort of shantytown hanging on the sides of the hills, with neither water nor light, where an impoverished population lives, Black and White. The women go to fetch water at the foot of the hills, where they line up and load their provisions into scrap-metal containers that they carry on their heads like Kabyle women. While they wait, an unbroken line of the silent, nickel-plated beasts of the American automobile industry passes in front of them. Never have luxury and misery seemed to me so insolently thrown together. It's true that, according to one of my companions, "they have a lot of fun, at least." Regret and

12 Gabrielle Mineur ("Mme. M.")—Worked in Cultural Services at the French Embassy in Brazil and helped arrange Camus's tour.

cynicism—B. alone is generous. He's going to take me to the favelas, which he knows well: "My beat as a reporter was the criminal and communist," he says. "Both good ways of getting to know the slums."

4°. People. Lunch with Mme. M., B., and a sort of thin, well-read, and witty lawyer, whose first name, Annibal,[13] is all I can remember, and for good reason, as we were in a country club that lives up to his name: tennis, lawns, young people. Annibal has six daughters, all pretty. He says the mixture of love and religion in Brazil is quite interesting. To a Brazilian hack who'd translated Baudelaire, he telegraphed: "Please translate me back to French immediately. Signed, Baudelaire." He reminds me of those many elegant Spaniards you meet deep in the provinces.

5°. One of the three or four Brazilian warships I've been shown, and which seems somewhat obsolete, is called *Terror do Mondo*. It's been through several revolutions.

6°. People. After lunch, reception at Mme. M.'s. Beautiful apartment on the harbor. The afternoon on the water is pleasant. Lots of people, but I've forgotten their names: a translator of Molière, who, a dear colleague tells me, added an act to *The Imaginary Invalid*, because it wasn't quite long enough to be performed; a Polish philosopher, from whom the heavens, if they be merciful, will protect me; a young French biologist on assignment, incredibly nice; most important, some young people from a troupe of Black actors who want to put on *Caligula*. I promise to work with them. Then, a side conversation with one of them who speaks Spanish, during which, with my dreadful Spanish, we arrange for me to attend a Black ball with him on Sunday. He's delighted with this little

13 Aníbal Machado (1894–1964)—Brazilian novelist and poet, elected president of the Brazilian Association of Writers in 1945. He organized the first Brazilian congress of writers in São Paulo.

With Abdias do Nascimento and members of his Teatro Experimental
do Negro at the Teatro Ginàstico in Rio de Janeiro. *Quilombo: vida,
problemas e aspirações do negro* 5, no. 11 (January 1950): 11.

prank we're going to pull on the officials and repeats: "Segreto.
Segreto."[14]

7°. When I think we're wrapping up, Mme. M. announces I'll
be dining with a Brazilian poet. I don't say a word, promising
myself that, starting tomorrow, I'll cut out everything that's
inessential. I resign myself. But I didn't expect the ordeal that
was to follow. The poet arrives, huge, indolent, squinty-eyed,
mouth hanging open.[15] From time to time, agitation, a sudden

14 The Spanish speaker mentioned here is Abidas do Nascimento (see p. 79n23,
below).

15 Augusto Frederico Schmidt (Federico) (1906–65)—Brazilian Modernist
poet and the founder and editor of Schmidt Editora, a publishing house important in the intellectual life of Rio between 1930 and 1939.

stirring, and then he spills himself back into his armchair and sits there panting a little. He gets up, pirouettes, and falls back into his armchair. He talks about Bernanos, Mauriac, Brisson, Halévy.[16] He knows everyone, apparently. They didn't treat him well. He doesn't take part in Franco-Brazilian politics, but he's founded a fertilizer plant with some French people. Anyway, he's never been honored. In this country, they honor all of France's enemies, but not him, no, etc., etc.

He momentarily drifts into dreams, visibly suffering from who knows what, then yields the floor to the señorito, who greedily takes it up, for this señorito is like those who proudly walked their long-legged dogs on the Calle Major in Palma de Mallorca[17] before setting out like connoisseurs to watch the executions of '36. This one here's the arbiter of all things: I just have to go see this, go do that, Brazil is a country where all we do is work, no vices, because who has the time, we work, we

16 Georges Bernanos (1888–1948)—French Catholic writer who emigrated to Brazil in 1938 and stayed until 1945.

François Mauriac (1885–1970)—French Catholic novelist and columnist for *Le Figaro* newspaper, frequently sparring with Camus over political and moral issues.

Henri Brisson (1835–1912)—French statesman who served twice as prime minister (1885–86 and 1898), known for his strong liberal and anti-clerical positions.

Daniel Halévy (1872–1962)—Historian known for an essay on the acceleration of history and for his conversion to right-wing ideology in the 1930s. The Brazilian poet Frederico Schmidt, one of Camus's hosts in Rio, befriended Halévy during his Paris years. The two men shared an appreciation of the French poet Charles Péguy.

17 Roger Quillot, an early Camus scholar and friend of the author, notes that this simile likely comes from a combination of personal experience, a trip Camus took to Mallorca in 1935, and a literary experience, his reading of Bernanos's *Les Grands Cimetières sous la lune* (*The Great Cemeteries beneath the Moon*), an eyewitness account of the violent nationalist repression in Mallorca during the years of the Spanish Civil War (Camus, *Œuvres Complètes*, vol. 4, ed. Raymond Gay-Crosier [Paris: Gallimard, 2008], 1550).

work, and Bernanos told him, and Bernanos created a lifestyle in this country, and oh how we love France so much ...

Frightened by the prospect of this event, I enlist the young biologist to come have dinner with us. In the car, I ask that we not go to a fancy restaurant. The poet emerges from his 330 pounds of weight to tell me, finger raised: "There is no luxury in Brazil. We're poor here, impoverished," he says, affectionately patting the tasseled shoulder of the chauffeur driving his enormous Chrysler. Having said this, the poet wearily sighs and returns to the recesses of his flesh, where he begins to absently gnaw at one of his complexes. The señorito shows us Rio, which is at the same latitude as Madagascar, yet so much more beautiful than Antananarivo.[18] "All workers," he repeats, sprawled in his cushioned seat. The poet has his driver stop in front of a pharmacy, laboriously pulls himself from the car, and asks us to hang tight a few minutes while he goes to get an injection. We wait, and the señorito comments: "Poor guy's diabetic." Letarget politely asks: "It's getting worse?"[19] Indeed. "Getting worse." The poet returns, whimpering, and collapses onto his poor cushioned seat, in his sad impoverished vehicle. We end up in a restaurant near Halles—where all you can get is fish—in a quadrangular room with a very high ceiling, the space so brutally lit with neon we look like pale fish gliding through irreal waters. The señorito wants to order for me. But, feeling drained, I'd prefer to eat lightly and so refuse everything he suggests. The poet is served first and he begins eating right away, without waiting for us, his fat and stubby

18 Antananarivo is the capital of Madagascar.
19 Raymond Latarjet (referred to here by Camus as Letarget) (1911–98)— French biologist who made important discoveries in oncology, virology, and radiobiology. He was a professor at the French National Institute for Nuclear Science and Technology and was elected to the French Academy of Sciences in 1976.

fingers sometimes taking the place of his fork. He talks about Michaux, Supervielle, Béguin, etc., interrupting himself from time to time to turn his nose up and spit bits and pieces of bone and fish out onto his plate.[20] This is the first time I've seen such a maneuver done without a person bending forward. He's so skilled at it, in fact, he misses his plate only once. Then the rest of us are served, and I see that the señorito ordered fried shrimp for me, which I turn down, explaining to him, in what I believe to be a friendly manner, that I'm familiar with the dish, a common one in Algeria. Hearing this, the señorito turns an angry red. We're only trying to make you happy, that's all. Humbly, in fact, humbly. You don't have to go looking all over Brazil for what you have in France, etc., etc. Fueled by my fatigue, a ridiculous anger washes over me, and I push my chair back to leave. A gentle intervention by Letarget, as well as the sympathy I feel, despite it all, for this curious character, the poet, holds me back, and I make a great effort to calm myself down. "Ah," the poet says, sucking his fingers, "Brazil requires a lot of patience, a lot of patience." All I say, as a retort, is that it didn't seem I'd been lacking it so far. Hearing this, the señorito calms down as quickly and senselessly as he'd gotten angry and, to try to make up, overwhelms me with compliments that leave me speechless: all Brazil feverishly awaits me, my visit to the country is the most important thing that's happened here for a long time, I'm as famous here as Proust ... There's no stopping him. He concludes with: "That's why you have to be patient with Brazil. Brazil needs your patience. Patience, well,

20 Henri Michaux (1899–1984)—Belgian-born poet, writer, and painter known for his unusual style often compared to Surrealism.

Jules Supervielle (1884–1960)—Franco-Uruguayan poet and writer who split his time between Montevideo and Paris.

Albert Béguin (1901–57)—Swiss literary critic and specialist in Romanticism; succeeded Emmanuel Mournier as head of the revue *Esprit*.

that's what Brazil requires ..." and so on. Despite it all, the rest
of the meal goes smoothly, though the poet and señorito continue to make asides in Portuguese, in which I believe they're
complaining about me a little. In fact, these rude manners are
spread out so naturally they become almost pleasantries. Leaving the restaurant, the poet declares that he needs a coffee and
that he'll drive us back afterward. We go to his club, which is
a copy of an English club, where I resign myself to drinking a
"real" cognac, which I don't want at all. The señorito takes the
opportunity to explain *Figaro*'s administrative difficulties to
us, which I know well, but of which he gives us an absolutely
false, peremptory description. Chamfort's right, though: if you
want to succeed in society, you have to let yourself learn a lot of
things you already know from people who don't know anything
about them. Nevertheless, I let them know I'm ready to go, but
not before the señorito has said, triumphantly, gesturing at the
poet, who's completely laid out in his armchair, his arm held
up like a periscope, gripping a monstrous cigar: "S. is Brazil's
greatest poet." To which the poet, faintly waving the periscope,
responds in a weary voice: "Brazil doesn't have a greatest poet."
I think I've made it through when, in the hall, the poet suddenly finds his second wind, violently grabs me by the arm, and
says: "Don't move a muscle. Pay close attention. I'll show you
a character for one of your novels." We notice a small, skinny
man on the sidewalk, fedora askew, features sharp. The poet
hurries toward him, swallows him in a long Brazilian embrace,
and says to me: "Now this is a man. A minister of the interior.
But a man." The man responds that Federico is excessively
kind. The señorito joins the show. Another embrace, on an
even footing this time, the señorito being a featherweight. The
señorito pulls the minister's jacket open: "Look." The minister
is carrying a revolver in a beautiful holster. We go on our way.

"He's killed some forty men," the poet says, filled with admiration. "Why? They were enemies."

Ah!

"One time, he killed a guy, then used the body as a shield and killed the others."

"He's allowed to carry a weapon," Letarget says, without flinching.

"Because he's a minister." Turning to me: "Is he not the perfect character for you?"

"Yes," I say. But he's wrong—he's the one who's the character.

*

July 16

Get up early. Work. I put my notes in order. Conversation with the waiter serving me. From Nice, wants to go to North America because he found the G.I.s friendly. He couldn't get an immigration visa, so he came to Brazil, thinking it would be easier to get the required visa here. It wasn't easier. I ask him what he wants to do in the U.S.A. He's hesitating between boxing and singing. For the time being, he's training to be a boxer. I'll go to the gym with him Monday.

Lunch with Barleto at a Brazilian novelist and translator's place.[21] She has a charming house hanging on a hill. Of course, there are a lot of people there, one of them a novelist who's sup-

---

21 João Batista Barreto Leite Filho (Barleto, B.) (1906–87)—Brazilian journalist and activist. He led the Union of Workers in Books and Newspapers (UTLJ) and was a member of the Brazilian Communist Party (PCB), though he challenged and criticized the Party for straying from Marxist principles to seize power. Between 1946 and 1949 he lived in Paris and Berlin as a war correspondent for the Associated Diaries, a conglomerate of Brazilian newspapers and radio stations.

posedly written the Brazilian *Buddenbrooks*, but who exhibits a curious case of half-formed cultural awareness. If I'm to believe B., the novelist was heard saying, "English authors like Shakespeare, Byron, or David Copperfield." Yet the novelist's clearly well-read, and as I couldn't care less if he mistakes David for Charles, I find him to have a rather good head on his shoulders. At lunch, a Brazilian couscous that turns out to be fishcakes. The guests are excited when I ask to attend a soccer match and absolutely ecstatic when they find out I had a long career playing soccer. I've inadvertently stumbled upon their true passion. But no, the hostess translates Proust, and everyone present has a truly deep understanding of French culture. Afterward, I ask B. if he wants to go for a walk with me in the city.

Traffic is forbidden on the smaller streets, cheerfully lit by multicolored signs, which are havens of peace next to the main thoroughfares of roaring traffic. It would be as if cars were forbidden on Rue Saint-Honoré between Concorde, Madeleine, and Avenue de l'Opéra. The flower market. The little bar where you drink "little coffees" sitting on tiny chairs. Moorish houses next to skyscrapers. Then Barleto makes me take a small "garden"-style tramcar, which climbs a steep path along the city's hills. We arrive in a neighborhood that's both poor and luxurious and that overlooks the city. In the dying light, the city stretches all the way to the horizon. A multitude of multicolored signs stand smoking above it. The outline of palm-tree-topped hills stands out against the calm sky. There's a tenderness in this sky, a fierce and barely concealed nostalgia. We take the stairs back down, and then walk through small and sloping streets, to reach the city itself. In the first real street that greets us, a positivist temple. They worship Clotilde de Vaux[22] here,

---

22 Auguste Comte (1798–1857) created what he called the Religion of Humanity or the Positivist Church, a fully formulated secular religion. It failed

and it's in Brazil that the most disconcerting thing Auguste
Comte left behind survives. A little farther along, a Gothic
church made of reinforced concrete. The temple itself is Greek,
but for lack of money, the columns remain without capitals. We
chat with B.N. in a little bistro. A charming man, sometimes
deep ("there's an innocence that's lost by sitting out in the sun
and darkening the skin"), who lives the drama of the times
with, it seems to me, great dignity. I leave him to meet up with
Abdias, the Black actor, at Mme. Mineur's. We'll leave for the
macumba from there.

A macumba, in Brazil

When I arrive at Mme. M.'s, there's an air of anxiety. The father of the saints (the priest and principal dancer), who was
to organize the *macumba*, consulted the saint of the day, who
didn't give his permission. Abdias,[23] the Black actor, thinks it's
mostly a matter of money, that he didn't promise enough to
earn the saint's goodwill. He thinks we should still take a trip
to Caxias, a village outside the city, 40 km from Rio, where we
might be able to find a macumba at random. During dinner,
they explain the macumbas to me. There seems to be a con-
sistent aim to the ceremonies: to coax the god down into the
body by means of song and dance. The goal is a trance. What

to catch on in France but found some success in Brazil. The temple Camus
mentions here is likely the Positivist Chapel in Porto Alegre.

Clotilde de Vaux (1815–46)—Comte's lover, who died a year into their relationship and who inspired Comte's religion and philosophy.
23 Abdias do Nascimento (1914–2011)—Founder of the Teatro Experimental do Negro, the Brazilian theater company preparing a production of
Caligula. The young Black actor accompanied Camus to Caxias, a suburb of
Rio, to attend a *macumba* performance. He also invited Camus to attend a
much-altered interpretation of a single act from *Caligula* on July 26, 1949, at
the Ginastico Theater (see pp. 97–98 below).

distinguishes the macumba from other ceremonies is its mix of Catholic religious practices and African rites. As far as gods or saints, they have Echou, an evil spirit and African god, as well as Ogoun, who is our Saint George. They have saints, too: Cosme and Damien, etc., etc. Here, the worship of saints is integrated with rites of possession. Each day has its own saint who's not celebrated on any other day, except with special permission from the principal "father of the saints." The father of the saints has his daughters (and his sons, I suppose), and he's responsible for making sure they've reached a trance.

Armed with this basic information, we head out. 40 km in a sort of fog. It's 10 at night. Caxias reminds me of a country fair composed of stands. We stop at the village square where there are already some twenty cars and a lot more people than we'd imagined. We have barely come to a stop when a young mulatto man hurries over to offer me a bottle of aguardiente,[24] asking if I've brought Tarrou with me. He has a good laugh— just kidding—and introduces me to his friends. He's a poet. Finally, they let me in on the fact that everyone in Rio knew I was going to be brought to see a macumba (I'd been told to keep it a secret and innocently did so) and that a lot of them wanted to come enjoy it. Abdias inquires about something, then sits still. We stay there, in the middle of the square, endlessly discussing this and that. No one seems to have a care in the world, everyone has their head in the stars. All of a sudden: a general hustling and bustling. Abdias tells me we have to go into the mountains. We set out, rolling along for a couple of kilometers on a bumpy road full of potholes, and then we suddenly stop for no clear reason. We wait, no one seeming to have a care in the world. Then we set out again. The car sud-

24 "Aguardiente" has traditionally been used in Latin America as a generic term for distilled alcohol.

denly veers off at a forty-five-degree angle and takes a mountain trail. It climbs, with difficulty, then stops: the path is too steep. We get out of the car and walk. The hill is smooth, the vegetation sparse, but we're up in the open sky, amid the stars, it seems. The air smells like smoke. It's so thick it almost feels like it's pressing against your forehead. When we reach the top of the hill, we can hear drums and singing off in the distance, but they stop almost immediately. We walk toward where we heard them. With neither trees nor houses, the place is a desert. But in a hollow we notice a sort of shed, rather spacious, without walls, its framework visible. Paper garlands are strung up along the shed. Suddenly, I notice a procession of Black girls climbing toward us. They're wearing white, dropped-waist dresses of coarse silk. A man dressed in a sort of red tabard, wearing necklaces of multicolored teeth, follows behind them. Abdias stops him and introduces me. The greeting is earnest and friendly. But there's a complication. They're going to join a different macumba that's a twenty-minute walk from here, and we'll have to follow them. We head out. At an intersection, I catch sight of a lit candle stuck in the ground, in a sort of niche where statues of saints or devils (quite crude, by the way, and in the style of Saint-Sulpice) are gathered in front of a tallow candle and a bowl of water. They point Echou out to me, red and fierce, with a knife in his hand. The path we're following snakes through the hills beneath a star-filled sky. The dancers, male and female, are in front of us, laughing and joking. We go down a hill, cross the trail by which we came, and climb back up another hill. Huts made of branches and clay, filled with whispering shadows. Then the head of the procession comes to a halt in front of a raised platform, surrounded by a partition of reeds. We can hear drums and singing inside. When we're all together, the first women climb onto the platform and step backward through the reed door. Then the men.

We enter a courtyard filled with junk. Singing escapes a small house of cob and straw in front of us. We enter. It's a very basic hut, the walls roughcast nevertheless. The roof is supported by a central mast, the floor is clay. A small lean-to in the back shelters an altar with a chromo print of Saint George above it. Similar chromos decorate the partitions. In one corner, on a small dais adorned with palm leaves, some musicians: two short drums and one tall drum. There were about forty dancers, men and women, when we arrived. Now there are so many of us we can hardly breathe, packed so tightly together. I back against one of the partitions and watch. The dancers, men and women, spread out into two concentric circles, the men on the inside. The two fathers of the saints (the one who received us is dressed, like the dancers, in a sort of white pajamas) face each other in the center of the circles. They take turns singing the first notes of a song everyone instantly takes up in chorus, the circles turning clockwise. The dance is straightforward: the double beat of a rumba played alongside a stomp. The "fathers" barely keep the rhythm. My Portuguese translator tells me these songs entreat the saint to allow newcomers to stay. The breaks between songs are rather long. Near the altar, a woman sings and shakes a bell so that it almost never stops. The dance is far from frenetic, its regular pattern fixed and heavy. In the still-increasing heat, the breaks are hard to bear. I notice:

1) that the dancers don't sweat the slightest bit;

2) a White man and two White women who dance much worse than the others.

At one point, one of the dancers comes over and speaks to me. My translator tells me the dancer's asking me to uncross my arms. The posture prevents the spirit from descending on us. Compliant, I let my arms drop. Little by little, the pauses between songs grow shorter and the dancing grows more spirited. A lit candle is brought to the center of the room and stuck

in the ground, near a glass of water. The songs invoke Saint
George.

"He arrives in the light of the moon
He departs in the light of the sun"

and then:

"I am the god's battlefield."

Indeed, one or two of the dancers already seem to be in a
trance, but, if I may say so, a calm trance: hands on their lower
back, standing straight, eyes blank and staring. The red "father" pours water around the candle in two concentric circles,
and the dancing resumes with almost no transition. From time
to time, one of the dancers, male or female, leaves the circle
to dance in the center, right by the circles of water, but never
crossing them. Their rhythm increases, they go into convulsions, and they begin to cry out inarticulately. Dust lifts from
the ground, suffocating, thickening air that already sticks to
the skin. The dancers increasingly leave their circles to dance
around the fathers, who themselves dance more quickly (the
White father, admirably). The drums are raging now and the
red father suddenly lets loose. Eyes ablaze, his four limbs whirl-
ing around his body, he lands on each leg in turn, knees bent,
his rhythm accelerating until the dance ends and he stops, gazing at the witnesses with a blank and terrible expression. Just
then, a dancer emerges from a dark corner, kneels, and holds a
sheathed sword out to him. The red father draws the sword out
and twirls it around his body in a threatening manner. A huge
cigar is brought to him. Little by little, everyone lights cigars
and smokes them while dancing. The dance resumes. One by
one, the witnesses come and lie down before the father, head

between his feet. He strikes them on each shoulder, in a diagonal, with the flat of the sword, lifts them up, touches their left shoulder with his right shoulder and vice versa; he pushes them violently into the ring, a movement that, two out of three times, sets off a fit, different for each dancer: a fat Black man stands on his heels, gazing at the central mast, a blank expression on his face, the only movement a shiver continually running the nape of his neck. He looks like a *knock down*[25] boxer. A thick White woman, face animalistic, barks continuously, shaking her head from right to left. But the young Black women enter the deepest trances, their feet glued to the ground, their entire body twitching with convulsions that grow more and more violent as they rise toward the shoulders. Their heads jerk back and forth, completely decapitated. Everyone whoops and screams. Then the women begin to fall. They're picked up, their foreheads are touched, and they're set loose until they fall again. The peak is reached when all cry out in strange, hoarse sounds reminiscent of barking. They tell me it'll keep going as it's been going all the way until dawn. It's 2 in the morning. The heat, the dust, the cigar smoke, and the human smell make the air unbreathable. I stagger outside, delighted to finally be breathing fresh air. I like the night and sky more than the gods of man.

*

July 17

Work in the morning. I have lunch with G. and two Brazilian professors. Three professors in all, but nice. Then, joined by

---

25 The phrase "knock down" is written in English in the original manuscript, though "punch-drunk" would be the more colloquial term.

Lucien Febvre,[26] a rather taciturn old man, we set out for a drive through the mountains surrounding Rio. Seen a hundred times, the Tijuca Forest, the Mayrink Chapel, the Corcovado, Guanabara Bay, every angle is completely different. The immense beaches of the South, with white sand and emerald waves, stretching across thousands of deserted kilometers, all the way to Uruguay. The rainforest and its three levels. Brazil is a land without people. Everything that's created here is created through excessive effort. Nature suffocates man. "Is space enough to create culture?" the nice Brazilian professor asks me. It's a meaningless question. But only these spaces measure up to technological progress. The faster the plane flies, the less importance France, Spain, and Italy hold. They were nations, are provinces, and tomorrow will be the world's villages. The future's not on our side, and there's nothing we can do about this irresistible trend. Germany lost the war because it was a nation and modern warfare requires the means of empires. Tomorrow, it'll require the means of a continent. So now the two great empires set out to conquer their continent. What's to be done? The only hope is that a new culture will be born and that South America may help to temper this mechanistic foolishness. So that's what I poorly expressed to my professor friend as we stood before the whistling sea, letting the sand run through our fingers.

I head back—having caught a chill while in the car and while under Christ the Redeemer—to wait for faithful Abdias, who's going to take me to dance the samba after dinner. Disappointing evening. In a neighborhood way on the outskirts, a sort of working-class dancehall brightly lit with neon,

26 Lucien Febvre (1878–1956)—Founder, with Marc Bloch, of the *Annales* school of historiography, he held the chair in modern history at the Collège de France from 1933 to 1949.

of course. There are, for the most part, only Black people—but that means a great variety of color here. Surprised by how slow they dance, with a sloshy sort of rhythm. But then I consider the climate. The manic dancers in Harlem would be duller here, too. Even so, nothing differentiates this dancehall from a thousand others around the world, except skin color. About that, I notice I have to fight a sort of reverse prejudice. I like Black people *a priori* and am tempted to find qualities in them that they don't have. I wanted to find the people here beautiful, but if I imagine their skin being White, what I find is more a pretty collection of calicos²⁷ and dyspeptic employees. Abdias confirms this. An ugly bunch. That said, among the mulatto women who come straight over to our table to have a drink, not because it's ours but because that's where you drink, one or two are pretty. I'm even sweet on the one who's losing her voice, dance a little bit of a samba with another woman, slap myself on the thighs to get myself going, and then suddenly realize I'm not into it. Taxi. I return to the room.

*

July 18

It's pouring rain over the steaming bay and over the city. Quiet morning of work. I go have lunch with Lage, in a cozy restaurant overlooking the harbor. At 3 o'clock, I meet up with Barleto to go visit the working-class suburbs. We take the commuter train. *Méier. Todos os santos. Madureira.*²⁸ What strikes me is its Arab feel. Shops without storefronts. Everything out

27 In colloquial French, "calicot" is used to refer to someone who works in a fabric shop.
28 Méier and Madureira are neighborhoods in the North Zone of Rio de Janeiro.

in the street. Saw a hearse: an Empire cenotaph with huge gilded bronze columns on a delivery van painted black. For the rich, it's horses. Striking fabrics on display. We take a bumpy tramcar that cuts through endless faubourgs that are empty most of the time, and sad (the tribes of workers camped at the entrance of the housing projects make me think of B.),[29] but as we get closer, they begin to coagulate around a central point, a square bright with neon, with red and green lights (in broad daylight), engulfed by a multicolored crowd at which a loud-speaker occasionally blares soccer scores. You can't help but think of these endlessly increasing crowds that'll end up covering the world's surface and suffocating. Here, I understand Rio better, better than in Copacabana, in any case, it's oily stain spreading infinitely in all directions. On the way back, in a *lotação*, a sort of public-transport taxi, we witness one of the many accidents occasioned by the unbelievable traffic. A poor old Negro man makes the mistake of trying to cross an avenue glittering with lights and is hit by a bus going full speed, is sent ten meters through the air, tossed like a tennis ball, and the bus just goes around him, fleeing the scene. It does so because of a stupid flagrante-delicto law on account of which the driver would have been taken to jail. So instead he flees, there's no longer any flagrante delicto, and he won't go to prison. The old Negro man lies there, not a single person coming to help him. But the blow would have killed an ox. Later, I learn a white sheet will be put over him, and it will grow soaked with blood, and candles will be lit around it, and the traffic will continue around him, bypassing him until the authorities arrive to re-construct the scene.

In the evening, dinner at Robert Claverie's. Only French people, which gives me a chance to relax. When you speak a

29 Probably Belcourt, Camus's childhood neighborhood in Algiers.

foreign language, there is, Huxley says, someone inside of you who automatically says no.[30]

*

July 19

Magnificent weather. A charming and myopic journalist. Mail. Lunch with the Delamains, in a sort of train-station buffet—neon lit, of course. Meal. Dark ruminations. As the afternoon comes to a close, I visit a drama school. Interview with students and teachers. Dinner at the Chapasses' with the national poet, Manuel Bandeíra, a small, extremely sharp man. Kaïmi, a Black man who composes and writes all the sambas sung in the country, sings and plays guitar after dinner.[31] They are the saddest, most moving songs. The sea and love, longing for Bahia. Little by little, everyone begins to sing, among them a Black man, a deputy, a college professor, a notary public, all naturally and gracefully singing along with these sambas. Totally seduced.

*

July 20

Morning in a motorboat on Guanabara Bay, the weather wonderful. Only a small, crisp wind lightly brushes over the wa-

---

30 Jean Robert Claverie—Head of the import-export company Maison d'importation Claverie and director of the Alliance Française in Rio.

Aldous Huxley (1894–1963)—English writer best known for his dystopian novel *Brave New World*.

31 Manuel Bandeíra (1886–1968)—Popular Brazilian poet at the time of Camus's visit.

Dorival Caymmi (Kaïmi) (1914–2008)—Brazilian singer and composer known as a founder of the bossa nova movement and for his many samba classics.

ter. We pass along the islands; some small beaches (two twins named Adam and Eve). Finally, a dip in the water, pure and fresh. Afternoon, visit from Murilo Mendès—poet, ill. Shrewd mind, resistant spirit. One of the two or three I've actually seen here. In the evening, a talk.[32] When I get there, the crowd is bottlenecked at the entrance. Claverie and the ravishing Mme. Petitjean[33] are already on their way out, not having been able to find seats. I find a pair for them, not without some difficulty. In the end, the auditorium, made to hold 800, is overflowing with listeners standing or sitting on the floor. Society people, diplomats, etc., arriving late, naturally, have to choose between standing or leaving. The Spanish ambassador sits on a riser behind the podium. In a few minutes, he'll learn a thing or two. Ninu, a Spanish refugee I knew back in Paris, bumps into me. He's head of the *campeones* on a fazenda 100 km from Rio. He came those 100 km to hear "*su compañero.*" He heads back tomorrow morning. When you consider what coming 100 km from the middle of nowhere means ... I'm moved to tears. Then he takes out a pack of cigarettes, the kind most like "*gusto frances,*" he says, and offers me one. I keep him close, happy to have such a friend in the auditorium, thinking it's for people like him I'll give this talk. So that is how I talk, and I've got men like N. on my side and, it seems, the other young people, too—but I doubt I have the society people on my side. Then, the mad dash. I collect a couple of sincere congratulations. The

32 The talk was given at the Itamaraty Palace, which housed the Ministry of Foreign Affairs.

33 Yvette Petitjean was one of the French expats living in Brazil who welcomed Camus. She and Camus visited the botanical gardens of Rio together and they became friends. She later visited him in Paris. In a December 1991 interview in the *French Review*, Petitjean gave the following impression of her time spent with Camus: "I found him extremely charming, a charmer, but also truly good, profoundly good, not full of himself. Albert Camus had the look of a little boy crossed with a Mandarin: young, good, and wise."

rest is playacting. Go to bed at midnight, having to get up at 4:30 A.M. to catch my flight to Recife.

*

July 21

Wake at 4:00 A.M. It's pouring rain. I get soaked just going from the embassy door to the taxi. At the air terminal, formalities, during which I'm asleep on my feet. Long way to the airfield. In this climate, you get soaked twice: first by the rain, then by your own sweat. At the airport, long wait. It turns out we won't take off until 8:30, and I again rage against the plane. While I wait, I look at a chart showing the distances between Rio and the world's capitals. Paris is almost 10,000 km away. Two minutes later, the radio plays *La vie en rose* for us. The plane takes off, heavy with rain, the sky low. I try to sleep but am unable to do so. When we land in Recife, four and a half hours later, the airplane door opens on a red land devoured by heat. It's clear we're at the equator again. Suffering from insomnia, vaguely feverish with some sort of cold I caught this morning, I stagger under the weight of the heat. Nobody is waiting for me. But it seems the plane is ahead of schedule, so it's not surprising. I wait in an empty hall, blazing air circling the room, and from afar contemplate the coconut forests surrounding the city. The delegation arrives. All nice. The three Frenchmen are all over six feet tall. We're well represented here. We get on our way. Red land and coconut trees. Then, the sea and its immense beaches. Hotel on the quay. Masts rising above the parapets. I try to sleep. In vain. Four hours. They come get me. The editor of the oldest newspaper in South America, *Le journal de Pernambouc*, is here. He's the one who's going to show me around the city. Admirable colonial churches dominated by white, the Jesuit style enlightened and lightened by roughcast. The interior is baroque, but without the excessive weight of the European Baroque. The Golden Chapel, in particular, is admirable. The *azulejos* are perfectly preserved here. As with the paintings, it's only the "wicked" Judases, the Roman soldiers, etc., that the people have disfigured. All of their faces are chewed and bloody. I admire the old town, the small red, blue, and ocher houses, the streets paved with large, pointed stones. The square of the church of San Pedro. The church, set next to a coffee factory, is completely blackened by smoke from the roasters. It's literally patinaed in coffee.

Dinner alone. The sound of an orchestra dying in the distance. Exile has its contentment. After dinner, a talk in front of a hundred or so people who appear exhausted as they leave. I like Recife, to be sure. A Florence of the Tropics, between its coconut-tree forests, its red mountains, its white beaches.

*

July 22

Get up with flu and fever. Legs unsteady. I get ready and wait at the hotel for three intellectuals who want to see me. Two likeable. We go see Olinda, a small, historic city with old churches, across from Recife, out on the bay. The Saint Francis convent is quite beautiful. On the way back, I shake with fever and swallow some aspirin and gin. Lunch at the consulate. After lunch, stroll along the sea, through a coconut-tree forest, where, through the openings, you can see, out on the sea, the sails of the *jangadas*, a type of narrow raft made from the trunks of a very light wood that's tied together with rope. These fragile assemblages take to the sea for days and days, I'm told. Straw huts scattered about. In the bright and suffocating air, the shadows of the coconut trees wobble before my eyes. The flu is getting worse, and I ask to rest before the interview at 5 o'clock. Impossible to sleep. A roundtable that I make it through thanks to two whiskies. Afterward, head over to a folk festival organized for me. They give me a flu shot. Uninteresting songs and dances. A phony macumba. But the *bomba-menboi*, extraordinary show. It's a sort of grotesque ballet danced by masked figures and totem-representations, the theme of which is always the same: the killing of an ox. The characters partly improvise on this theme and partly recite a text written in verse, all while dancing. The part I see goes on for an hour, but I'm told it could go on all night. The costumes are extraordinary. Two red clowns, the "cavalier marin,"[34] a merry-go-round horse costume draped from his shoulders, a stork, a braggart dressed as a cowboy, two Indians, the ox, of course, and a "dead person carrying a live one," a sort of double-bodied mannequin controlled by a single actor, the *cachaça* (or drunkard), the horse's son, a prancing colt, a man on stilts, a crocodile, and, hanging over everything, death, at least three meters tall, looking out over the scene, its head high in the night sky. As an orchestra, a drum and rumba box. The religious origin is obvious (a few prayers still linger in the text), but it's all drowned in a frenzied dance,

34 The performance Camus attended in Recife was a *bumba meu-boi*, from *bumba* meaning a call to action (but alluding also to the bomba drum) and *meu-boi* meaning "my ox." The performance tells the story of life on the sugar plantations and features the Captain, a member of the Euro-Brazilian ruling class, who comes to seize the property of the workers, men of color, by force. The dancing is frenzied, and the figures—ox, stork, cowboys, Cavalier Marin—wear elaborate costumes, mixing the animal and the human. In the grand finale, the performers would have cried out, "Viva Senhor Camus e o Santo Rei do Oriente," meaning "Long live Mr. Camus and the Holy King of the East" (i.e., Jesus Christ), which Camus and his party hear as "Camus and the Kings of the Orient." For a history of the *bumba meu-boi*, see John Patrick Murphy, *Music in Brazil: Experiencing Music, Expressing Culture* (Oxford: Global Music Series, Oxford University Press, 2006), 71–86.

a thousand graceful or grotesque feats that conclude with the killing of the ox, which is reborn shortly afterward and gallops off carrying a little girl between its horns. The grand finale: a great cry, "Long live Señor Camus and the hundred *kings* of the Orient." I go back to the hotel, dazed by the flu.

*

July 23

9 o'clock. Depart for Bahia. My flu is a little better. But I'm still feverish and stiff. It's cold in the plane, God knows why? And it shakes terribly. Three hours in the air, then short hills covered in snow appear over a great stretch of land. At least that's the impression the white sand, so widespread here, gives me, its immaculate waves seeming to surround Bahia in an untouched desert. From the airfield to the city, six kilometers of winding road running between banana trees and dense vegetation. The land is completely red. Bahia, where you see only Black people, seems like an immense and bustling casbah, impoverished, dirty, and beautiful. Excessively large marketplaces made of torn sails and old boards, of short, old houses plastered with red, green-apple, and blue lime, etc.

Lunch on the harbor. Large boats with ocher and blue lateen sails unload bunches of bananas. We eat dishes spicy enough to cause miracles in paralytics. The bay, which I can also see from my hotel window, stretches out beneath a gray sky, round and clear, full of a strange silence, while the motionless sails you see out there look as if they're imprisoned in a suddenly frozen sea. I prefer this bay to the one in Rio, too spectacular for my taste. This one, at least, has its limits and its poetry. Since morning, downpours, one after the other, brutal and abundant. They've turned the potholed streets of Bahia into torrents. We drive between two great blades of water that continuously cover the car.

Visit some churches. They're the same as in Recife, even if these are supposedly more famous. Church of the Good Jesus with its votive offerings (casts, pair of buttocks, X-ray, brigadier stripes). Suffocating. This harmonious baroque is repeated again and again. In the end, it's the only thing to see in this country, and it's seen quickly. Real life is what remains. But in this immeasurable land that holds the sadness of wide-open spaces, life is lived close to the ground and it would take years to become a part of it. Do I wish to spend years in Brazil? No. At six o'clock, I take a shower, fall asleep, and wake up a little better. Dine alone. Then a talk given to a patient audience. The consul escorts me and slips, under the table, after the last drink, an envelope containing around 45,000 fr in Brazilian currency. It's the honorarium given by the University of Bahia. The consul is surprised by my refusal. He explains to me that "others demand such an honorarium." Then he accepts my position. Still, I know he won't be able to help thinking: "If he needed it, he'd accept it." And yet ...

Before finishing, I copy down a couple of passages from the Palace Hôtel de Bahia's rules and regulations, which are written in French: "Everybody speaks French in Brazil," the propaganda says.

"Failure to pay bills, as stipulated in par. 3 and 4, will oblige management to withhold luggage as a guarantee against debt, and accordingly the client will immediately unoccupy the occupied room."

"It's forbidden to possess birds, dogs, or other animals in your room."

"On the ground floor of the hotel, you will find a well-stocked American bar and a spacious reading room."

And here's the one they end with:

"On the ground floor of the hotel, there is a barbershop and nail salon.

Clients may request the use of these services in their own room."

✳

July 24 (Sunday)

At ten o'clock, a charming Brazilian, Eduardo Catalao,[35] polite as can be, takes me to Itapoa beach by way of a potholed road. It's a fishing village made up of straw huts. The beach is beautiful and wild, the sea frothy at the foot of the coconut trees. This never-ending flu brings me to my knees and prevents me from swimming. We come across a group of young French filmmakers living in a straw hut so they can make a film about Bahia. Surprised to see me in this lost corner of the world. They have an air of Saint-Germain-des-Prés about them.

Scathing lunch at three o'clock. From 5:00 to 7:00, I work. Dinner at the consul's. Then we go see a candomblé, a new ceremony belonging to that curious Afro-Brazilian religion that, here, is Black Catholicism. It's a sort of dance performed in front of a table loaded with food, to the sound of three increasingly large drums and a flattened funnel struck with an iron rod. The dances are directed by a sort of matron, who takes the place of the "father of saints," and are performed only by women. The costumes are much richer than in Bahia. Two of the dancers, who are, by the way, enormous, have their faces covered with a curtain of raffia. Still, not much of this is new to me until a group of Black girls enters the scene in a semi-hypnotic state, eyes practically closed, yet standing upright,

35 Eduardo Catalão (1912–2004)—Brazilian agronomist and politician who served as minister of agriculture between 1955 and 1956.

swaying on their feet, back and forth. I'm taken with one of them, tall and thin, wearing a blue huntress's hat with musketeer feathers, its brim turned up, and a green dress, while holding in her hand a green and yellow bow equipped with an arrow, a multicolored bird skewered on its tip. This beautiful, sleeping face reflects a symmetrical and innocent melancholy. This Black Diana is of infinite grace. When she dances, that extraordinary grace is undeniable. Still asleep, she staggers as the music stops. The rhythm alone acts as a sort of invisible stake around which she winds her arabesques, occasionally uttering a strange birdcall, piercing yet melodious. The rest isn't that great. Watered-down rites expressed in mediocre dances. We leave with Catalao. In this remote neighborhood, as we stumble through the potholed streets, through the heavy, aromatic night, the cry of the injured bird still reaches out to me, reminding me of my sleeping beauty.

I'd like to go to bed, but Catalao wants to have a whisky at one of those sad-as-death nightclubs you find all over the world. Without my knowing, he asks for some French music, and for the second time, I hear *La vie en rose* in the Tropics.

*

July 25

Wake up at 7 o'clock. Have to wait for a plane that may not come. Then, it's confirmed. I'll leave at 11:00. My flu's getting better, but my legs are still cottony. Furious desire to go home. Two hours lost at the airfield. We leave. It's 1:30, and we won't arrive in Rio before 7 o'clock. I'm writing all of this on the plane, where I feel quite lonely.

Evening. Flu and fever return with a vengeance upon arrival. This time, it seems serious.

*

July 26

In bed. Fever. Only the mind stubbornly persists. Awful thoughts. Unbearable feeling of walking step by step toward an unknown catastrophe that will destroy everything around and inside of me.

Evening. They come get me. I'd forgotten that the Black troupe was going to put on an act from *Caligula* for me tonight. The theater has already been reserved, there's nothing to be done. I wrap myself up as if I were going to the North Pole and take a taxi to the theater.

Odd to see Black Romans. Then, what I'd seen as a cruel and intense way of acting becomes a slow, tender, vaguely sensual flirtation. After this, they put on a short Brazilian play that's just perfectly to my taste. I'll give the gist of it:

"A man, used to taking part in macumbas, is visited by the spirit of love. He then throws himself on his wife, who's transported and falls in love with the spirit. So she provokes, with the same song, the coming of the spirit as often as she can, which gives a pretext for putting some lively bacchanals on stage. In the end, the husband understands that it's not him she's in love with but the God, and he kills her. She dies happy, however, because she's certain she's going to the God she loves."

The evening ends with some Brazilian music that seems mediocre. Important, still, because Brazil may be the only predominately Black country that continuously produces new tunes. The highlight is a *frevo*,³⁶ a dance from Pernambuco, in

36 The term *frevo* is used to describe the various styles of music and dance most traditionally associated with Brazilian Carnival.

which the audience themselves take part and which is really the most frenzied contortion I've seen. Charming. Barely back to my room, I hit the bed and sleep like a rock, not waking until 9 o'clock in the morning, infinitely better.

*

July 27

Brazil, with its thin framework of modernity laid over this immense continent teeming with natural and primitive forces, makes me think of a building slowly chewed, bite by bite, by invisible termites. One day the building will collapse, and a small and teeming people, Black, red, and yellow, will spread out over the surface of the continent, masked and brandishing spears, ready for the victory dance.

Lunch with the poet Murilo Mendès—a sharp and melancholy mind—his wife, and a young poet who's collected 17 fractures and a pair of crutches thanks to Rio's intelligent traffic system.[37] After lunch, they take me to Sugarloaf. But the morning is spent waiting in line only to get no closer, in the end, than the first piton—to the great dismay of Mme. Mendès, who's afraid I'm bored, even though, in their friendly company, I'm in a good mood. M. knows and quotes Char, whom he finds to be our most important poet since Rimbaud.[38] I'm happy to hear that.

---

37 Murilo Mendes (1901–75)—Brazilian Modernist poet who later converted to Catholicism and wrote mystical verse. His wife, Maria da Saudade Cortesão (1913–2010), was a poet and translator of T. S. Eliot, Shakespeare, and, in 1963, Camus's *Caligula*. René Char (1907–88), poet and member of the French Resistance, was Camus's close friend and soon-to-be-neighbor in Provence; Camus first visited Char in Isle-sur-la Sorgue in 1946.

38 Arthur Rimbaud (1854–91)—French poet who famously stopped writing poetry at age twenty, known for *A Season in Hell* and *Illuminations*.

*

July 28

The Embassy of Montevideo complicates my stay by wanting to change the previously arranged dates. In the end, I'll be staying in Rio until Wednesday before going to São Paulo. Lunch with Simon and Barleto, whom I like more and more each day. The afternoon is spent working. In the evening, a reception at the embassy, which, however charming, bores me. I take French leave, as they say here, and go to bed.

*

July 29

The days in Rio have little rhyme or reason and pass both fast and slow. Lunch with Mme. B. and her sister-in-law. French women make for good company. Lively, witty, the time passes quickly. Stroll afterward, along the bay, the day marvelous and relaxed. It's difficult to tear myself away from these easy, natural moments only to have to run off to the embassy to find Mendès and his wife, who are going to take me to Corrêa's, the ex-publisher, where I have to meet with a student who ..., etc. What I've persistently refused my whole life, I accept here—as if I'd agreed in advance to do everything on this trip I don't want to do. I get out in time to meet up with Claverie, Mme. B., and her sister-in-law,[39] whom I've invited to dinner. After dinner, Claverie takes us for a ride on roads that cut through the mountains and into the night. The warm air, the stars, so

39 Mme. Jeannette Besse ("Mme. B") and her sister-in-law, the previously mentioned Mme. Yvette Petitjean, French expatriates who welcomed Camus to Brazil.

many tiny specks, the bay far below ... but it all makes me more melancholy than happy.

*

July 30 and 31

Weekend at Cl.'s in Teresópolis. 150 km from Rio, up in the mountains. The route is beautiful, especially between Petrópolis and Teresópolis. From time to time, an ipe[40] covered in yellow flowers jumps out from around a corner, against a horizon of mountains following one after the next, all the way out to the horizon. It's easy to again understand here what first struck me in the plane while I was flying over the country. Immense stretches, virgin and solitary, out of which the cities, hung on the coast, appear as nothing but unimportant dots. At any moment, this enormous, unpaved continent, entirely given over to natural wilderness, could turn and take back these cities of false luxury. The weekend is spent walking, swimming, and playing ping-pong. I can finally breathe out here in the countryside. The air at 800 m. helps me get a better sense of Rio's climate, truly exhausting. When we head back down on Sunday, it's without joy that I return to the city. On top of that, I'm greeted in front of the embassy by one of those scenes that are all too frequent in Rio. Again, a woman lying bloodied in front of a bus. A crowd looking on in silence, without trying to help her. This barbaric custom is revolting. A long time passes before I hear an ambulance siren. The whole time, they left the poor, moaning woman out there

---

40 The most likely interpretation here is that Camus has abbreviated the French "ipéca," itself an abbreviation of "ipécacuanha," the name of the plant from which ipecac syrup is derived.

to die. Yet they turn around and make a big pretense of adoring children.

*

August 1

Difficult waking up. To live is to hurt—to hurt others and yourself through others. Cruel land! How not to touch anything? What permanent exile is there?

Lunch at the embassy. I'm told the death penalty is unheard of in Brazil. In the afternoon, a talk about Chamfort.[41] I always wonder why I attract socialites. All those hats! Dinner with Barleto, Machado, etc., in a nice Italian restaurant. In the afternoon, we visit a favela. A number of long negotiations before entering the city, a genuine city, made of wood and tin and reeds, clinging to the side of a hill above Ipanema beach. Finally, we're told we can go for a consultation (as a letter of introduction, we have, it's true, two good bottles of cachaça) with one of the ladies of the place. We enter at night, between shacks emitting the sounds of either radios or snoring. The ground is completely vertical in spots, slippery, cluttered with garbage. It takes a good fifteen minutes to reach, out of breath, the Pythia's shack.[42] But as we stand on the platform in front of the shack, our effort is rewarded: beneath a half-moon, the

41 Nicolas Chamfort (1741–94)—French writer known for his aphorisms. In 1944, Camus had written an introduction for Nicolas Chamfort's *Maximes et anecdotes*, parts of which he adapted for the talk he gave at the Ministry of Foreign Affairs in Rio. The talk has sometimes been titled "Chamfort: Moralist of Rebellion" and sometimes "Rebellion and the Novel," the latter title also given to a section of *The Rebel* in which he expanded on the central ideas of the talk.

42 The Pythia was the name given to the priestess serving as Oracle of Delphi.

beach and the bay stretch out before us, still and motionless. It seems the Pythia is asleep. Then she opens up for us. The shack is like a lot of others I've seen, with multicolored strips of cloth hanging from the ceiling. In one corner, a bed with someone asleep in it. In the middle, a red curtain covers a table with laundry on it, making it look like there's a dead body underneath. In an alcove with an altar, all the statues of saints that Saint-Sulpice has exported throughout the world are gathered. Also, a Red-Skin statue, lost there, who knows how. The Pythia seems like a fine homemaker. She's just finished the day's consultations, which she gives only when the saint is in her. The saint is gone now. It'll have to wait until next time. It's hot. Still, the Black people here are so welcoming and affable that we stay and chat a while longer. The descent, a real race toward death. Imagine what it's like for the women who go two or three times a day to fetch water, a bucket atop their head as they climb back up. Imagine what it's like on rainy days. As it is, Barleto takes a one-way ticket to the ground floor. I reach the bottom, safe and sound, and we end the evening at Machado's. He tells me about death's assistants out in Minas.⁴³ In some cases, when the agony goes on too long, these licensed gentlemen are summoned. They arrive, dressed as funeral directors, nod, take off their gloves, and go to the dying person. They ask the person to pray "Mary-Jesus" and not to stop, while they place a knee on the person's stomach and their hands over the person's mouth and apply pressure until the sufferer drifts over the edge. They step back, put their gloves back on, receive fifty cruzeiros, and leave surrounded by a general sense of gratitude and respect.

43 Minas Gerais is a large state at the southern end of Brazil and the country's central hub of coffee production.

*

August 2

Tired of making notes about nothing. (I'm writing this in the plane to São Paulo. Yesterday was a whole lot of nothing. Even a conversation with Mendès about the relationship between culture and violence, which helped me sharpen my thinking, seemed like another nothing.)

Haunted, in reality, in the glorious light of Rio, by the thought of the harm we do to others the moment we look at them. Causing suffering has long been a thing of indifference to me, I have to admit. It's love that's enlightened me about this. Now, I can no longer bear it. In a way, it's better to kill than to cause suffering.

What finally seemed clear to me yesterday is that I wish to die.

*

August 3

Night falls fast in São Paulo, bright signs atop thick skyscrapers lighting up one by one while thousands of birds greet the end of the day from the royal palms that stand tall between the buildings, the steady birdsong covering the deep bass of the car horns that announce the return of the businessmen.

Dinner with Oswald de Andrade, a remarkable character (expand on this later). From his point of view, Brazil is peopled with primitives and is all the better for it.

The city of São Paulo, a strange city, an outsized Oran.

I stupidly forgot to note the thing that touched me most. A radio show in São Paulo where poor people come on to discuss

Camus arrives in São Paulo, August 2, 1949. Photo:
Acervo/Estadão. Courtesy of Estadão Conteúdo.

their needs given their current situation. This evening, a tall, poorly clothed Negro man, a 5-month-old little girl in his arms, baby bottle in his pocket, came on to explain that, quite simply, his wife had abandoned him and he was looking for someone who could take care of the child without taking it away from him. An ex-fighter pilot, out of work, looking for a job as a mechanic, etc. Then, in the offices, we wait for listeners' phone calls. Five minutes after the end of the broadcast, the phone rings off the hook. Everyone offers themselves or offers something. While the Black man is on the line, the ex-pilot holds the child and cradles her. And the best part: a tall, much older Negro man enters the office half-dressed. He was sleeping and his wife, who was listening to the show, woke him and told him: "Go get the child."

*

August 4

Press conference in the morning. Lunch standing up at Andrade's. At 3 o'clock, they take me, I don't really know why, to the city penitentiary, "the most beautiful in Brazil." It is, in fact, "beautiful," like a penitentiary in an American film. Except the smell, the awful smell of man that lingers in every prison. Bars, iron doors, bars, doors, etc. And as you get deeper inside, signboards: "Be good" and above all "Optimism." I'm ashamed standing there in front of one or two of the prisoners, who are themselves among the privileged, and who are doing some work for the prison. The doctor-psychiatrist then begins to check off all the categories of mental perversity, and in doing so drives me up a wall. Someone tells me, as we're leaving, the standard slogan: "Here, you're at home."

I forgot. On our way there, we passed through a street filled with prostitutes. They stand behind doors with vertical blinds, the gaps between the slats wide enough to see them, charming for the most part, in any case. You discuss the price through the slats, which are painted in all imaginable colors, green, red, yellow, sky blue. They're caged birds.

Then, a steep climb up a small skyscraper. São Paulo at night. The fairytale side of modern cities, glittering roofs and avenues. Cafés and orchids all around. It's hard to imagine, though.

Then Andrade tells me about his theory: cannibalism as a vision of the world.[44] Faced with Descartes's failure and the failure of science, a return to primitive fertilization: matriarchy and cannibalism. Given that the first bishop who landed in Bahia was eaten there, Andrade dates his manifesto Year 317 of the Swallowing of Bishop Sardine (for his name was Sardine).

Last hour. After my talk,[45] Andrade tells me that in that model penitentiary, you see prisoners commit suicide by smashing their head against the walls or closing a drawer on their throat until they suffocate.

*

44 Oswald de Andrade (1890–1954), poet and Brazilian Modernist intellectual, was the author of *The Cannibalist Manifesto*, published in 1928, in which he criticizes Europe's destructive influence on Brazil and argues that by "cannibalizing" other cultures—which is to say assimilating them—Brazil would create its own unique postcolonial identity. The aptly named Fernandes Sardinha (i.e., Sardine), appointed the first Catholic bishop of Brazil, was slaughtered and cannibalized there in 1556.
45 This was the "Time of the Murderers" talk that Camus gave several times during his tour of South America—a precursor to *The Rebel*. The talk is included in the collection *Speaking Out: Lectures and Speeches*.

August 5, August 6, August 7 (Trip to Iguape)

We leave for the religious festivals in Iguape, but at 10 o'clock instead of at 7, as we'd planned. In fact, we were supposed to drive through the interior, on Brazil's pothole-filled roads, during the day, as it's best to arrive before night. There was a delay, though, the car wasn't ready, etc. We leave São Paulo and begin the drive south. The roads, whether of earth or stone, are consistently covered in a red dust that blankets all the vegetation for a kilometer on either side of the road in a layer of dry mud. After a couple of kilometers, we ourselves—which is to say the driver, who looks like Auguste Comte, Andrade and his son, who's responsible for philosophers, Sylvestre, the French cultural attaché, and myself—are covered in the same dust.[46] It seeps in through every crack and crevice of our big Ford truck and little by little fills our mouths and noses. Overhead, a ferocious sun roasts the earth, bringing all life to a halt. Fifty kilometers on, a sinister noise. We stop. One of the front springs is broken, very clearly having escaped from its housing and now rubbing against the wheel rim. Auguste Comte scratches his head and declares that we'll be able to get it fixed in about twenty kilometers or so. I advise him to remove the casing now before it gets caught against the tire. He's an optimist, though. Five kilometers farther and we have to stop, the spring being caught. Auguste Comte decides to get a tool, which is to say he takes a tire iron from the trunk and uses it like a hammer, repeatedly striking the casing, claiming that it'll come off with a little force.

I explain there's a nut that needs to be removed and then there's the wheel itself. Then I finally realize he's set out on this

---

46 On the real Auguste Comte, see p. 78n22 above.

long journey over pothole-filled paths without even a monkey wrench. We wait there, beneath a sun that could slay an ox— and finally a truck drives by and the driver, thankfully, has a monkey wrench. The wheel removed, the nut loosened, the casing is finally removed. We set off again between the pale, furrowed mountains, encountering, sometimes, a starving zebu, escorted at other times by sad black-vultures. At 1 o'clock, we arrive in Piédade, an unsightly little village where we're warmly welcomed by the innkeeper, Dona Anesia, whom Andrade must have courted at one point. Served by a Métis Indian, Maria, who ends up offering me artificial flowers. An interminable Brazilian meal that we get through thanks to pinga, which is what they call cachaça here. We set off again, the spring having been repaired. We're continually ascending and the air is getting very dry. There are immense expanses of uninhabited, uncultivated land. The terrible solitude of this outsized stretch of nature goes a long way in explaining things about this country. Arrived in Pilar at 3 o'clock. Once we're there, August Comte realizes he's made a mistake. We're told we've gone 60 kilometers too far. On these roads, that means two or three hours of driving. Aching from all the bumping and shaking, covered in dust, we set back out to find the right path. In reality, we don't begin to descend the Serra until the end of the day. I have time to see the first kilometers of the rainforest, the thickness of that vegetal sea, to imagine the solitude that exists in the center of that unexplored world, night falling as we sink deeper into the forest. We roll on for hours, pitched this way and that on a narrow road running between high walls of trees, surrounded by a faintly sugary scent. In the thick of the forest, lightning bugs—illuminated flies—flicker here and there, and red-eyed birds come and beat against the windshield for only a second. Aside from this, the stillness and silence of this terrifying world are absolute, even if Andrade sometimes claims to hear a leopard. The road twists and turns, passing wobbly-planked bridges stretched across small rivers. Then the mist comes and a fine rain dissolves our headlights. We're no longer driving, but literally creeping. It's almost 7 in the evening, we've been driving since 10 in the morning, and our fatigue is such that we welcome, with fatalism, the hypothesis Auguste Comte presents: we may run out of gas. Nevertheless, the forest begins to thin a little—and slowly, the landscape begins to change. Finally, we come out into the open air and arrive in a small village where we're stopped by a large river. Light beacons from the other side and then we see a large ferry arriving, the oldest system there is, with poles steered by mulattos in straw hats. We embark and the ferry drifts slowly over the Ribeira River. The river is wide and flows gently toward the sea and night. On both banks, the forest remains thick. In the soft sky, stars enveloped in mist. Everyone aboard goes quiet. The absolute silence of the hour is disturbed only by the river lapping at the sides of the ferry. At the front of the ferry, I watch the river flow, the scene strange yet familiar. From both banks, weird bird cries and cane-toad croaks. It's midnight in Paris, at this exact moment.

Debarking. Then we continue to creep toward Registro, an authentic Japanese capital in the center of Brazil, where I get a chance to glimpse a few delicately decorated houses and even a kimono. We're told, then, that Iguape is only 60 km away.

We set out again. A humid breath of air and incessant drizzle let us know we're not far from the sea. The road itself turns to sand—more difficult and dangerous than it was before. It's 12:00 A.M. when we finally arrive in Iguape. Not counting all our stops, it took us ten hours to travel the 300 km now separating us from São Paulo.

The hotel is all closed up. A prominent citizen we run into in the night takes us to the mayor's house (the prefect, they say here). The mayor informs us, through the door, that we're to sleep at the hospital. Off to the hospital. Despite the exhaustion, the city seems beautiful, with its colonial churches, the nearby forest, the low, bare houses, and the softness of the dripping-wet air. Andrade claims he can hear the sea. But it's far away. At the "Happy Memory" hospital (that's its name), the friendly prominent citizen leads us to an unused ward, which smells like fresh paint, even from a hundred yards away. He tells me that, in fact, it's been repainted in our honor. But there's no light, as the country's power plant stops running at 11 o'clock. Nevertheless, in the glow of our lighters, we glimpse six clean and rustic beds. This is our dormitory. We set our bags down. The prominent citizen wants us to have a sandwich at the club. Completely worn out, we go to the club. The club is a sort of bistro on the second floor where we meet other prominent citizens who shower us with respect. I once again note the Brazilians' exquisite politeness, a little ceremonious perhaps, but still so much better than the Europeans' boorishness. Sandwich and beer. A tall beanpole of a man who can barely keep himself upright has the bright idea of coming over to ask me for my passport. I show it to him and it seems he's saying my papers aren't in order. Exhausted, I tell him to take a hike. The prominent citizens, indignant with the man, hold a sort of board meeting, after which they tell me they're going to put the policeman (for he is one) in prison and that I have to choose what charges to press. I ask them to please set him free. They explain that the great honor I'm doing Iguape hasn't been properly recognized by this loudmouth and that such a lack of manners must be sanctioned. I protest. But they're determined to do me this honor. The whole thing goes on until the next evening when I finally find the right way of putting it to them, asking if they'd do me the exceptional, personal favor of sparing this thoughtless individual. They buzz about my chivalry and tell me things will be taken care of according to my wishes.

In any case, the night of this drama we set off for the hospital, surrounded by kindness, and halfway there we run into the mayor, who got up and came over to personally lead us to our beds. He's also woken the power plant's personnel and now we have light. They get us settled in, they practically tuck us in, and finally, at 1 o'clock, completely worn out, we all try to go to sleep at the same time. I say try because my bed tilts a little and my neighbors turn back and forth and Auguste Comte snores ferociously. At last, I drift off, late at night, to a dreamless sleep.

*

August 6

Wake up very early. Unfortunately, no water in the hospital. I shave with mineral water and do a little washing up in the same way. Then the prominent citizens arrive and lead us to the main ward to have something to eat. Finally, we head out into Iguape.

In the small Fontaine Garden, mysterious and gentle, with bunches of flowers between banana and pandan trees, I'm able to relax a little and find some calm. Some Métis, some mulattos, and the first gauchos I've seen are waiting patiently in front of the entrance to a grotto where they'll receive shards of the Stone That Grows. In fact, Iguape is the city of the Good Jesus, whose effigy was found out on the waves by some fishermen who washed it in this grotto. Since then, a stone has continued to grow there, and they chip pieces of it off, highly beneficial. The city itself, between the forest and the river, is gathered around the Church of the Good Jesus. A few hundred houses, but with a unique style, low, roughcast, multicolored. Beneath a fine rain soaking the poorly paved streets, with the motley crew filling it—Japanese, Indians, Métis, elegant prominent citizens—Iguape bears the colonial stamp. You breathe a very particular melancholy there, the melancholy of the far ends of the world. Aside from the heroic route we took, the only thing linking Iguape and the rest of the world is two weekly planes. You can withdraw from the world here.

Throughout the day, our hosts' kindness never wavers. But it's the procession we've come to see. As soon as afternoon arrives, firecrackers begin to go off everywhere, causing the hairless vultures perched on the rooftops to fly off. The crowd thickens. Some of these pilgrims have been traveling the pothole-filled paths of the interior for five days. One of them, who has the look of an Assyrian, with a beautiful black beard, tells us that the Good Jesus saved him from a shipwreck, after he'd spent a day and night out on the raging waters, and that he's vowed to carry a 60 kg stone on his head throughout the procession. The hour draws near. From the church come Black penitents, then White, wearing surplices, then angel-children, then something like the Children of Mary, then the effigy of the Good Jesus himself, behind which the bearded man moves forward, torso naked, carrying an enormous slab on his head. Finally, the orchestra comes out playing "double time," and then to finish up, the crowd of pilgrims, the only interesting group, really, the rest being rather sordid and ordinary. The crowd lining the narrow street, overflowing it, is really the strangest gathering you could find. Ages, races, clothing color, classes, disabilities, all mixed together in a swaying and colorful mass, starred, sometimes, with tapers, above which firecrackers continually explode and, every now and again, a plane passes, unusual in this ageless world. Mobilized for the occasion, the planes roar at regular intervals above the elegant prominent citizens and the Good Jesus. We go to another strategic position to wait for the procession, and as it passes in front of us, the bearded man appears tensed with exhaustion, his legs trembling. Nevertheless, he makes it to the end safely. The bells ring, the houses and shops along the processional route that had closed their doors and windows reopen them—and we go for dinner.

After dinner, some gauchinos sing in the square and everyone sits around them. The firecrackers continue and a child blows off a finger. He screams and cries as he's led away: "Why'd the Good Jesus do this?" (They translate this soul-cry for me.)

To bed early because we leave early the next day. But the firecrackers, along with Auguste Comte's terrific sneezing, keep me from falling asleep until late at night.

*

August 7

Same route, except we avoid the other day's detour and cross three rivers. Saw some hummingbirds. I again gaze, for hours, at the monotonous nature and immense spaces, which you can't quite call beautiful but which stick to the soul in an insistent way. A country where the seasons blend together, one with the other, where the vegetation is so tangled as to become shapeless, where blood is mixed to the point the soul has lost its limits. A heavy swishing sound, the forest's murky blue-green light, the varnish of red dust covering everything, time melting, the slow pace of rural life, the brief and senseless excitement of big cities—this is a land of indifference and bloodshed. No matter how it tries, the skyscraper hasn't yet conquered the forest's spirit, its immensity, its melancholy. It's the sambas, the real ones, that best express what I mean.

The last fifty kilometers are the most exhausting. August Comte, cautious, lets everyone else pass. But then each car lifts so much red dust into the air that the headlights are no longer able to penetrate the mineral fog and the car has to stop sometimes. We don't know where we are anymore, and my mouth and nostrils feel like they're stuffing up with a suffocating mud. I welcome, with relief, São Paulo, the hotel, a hot bath.

*

August 8

All these degrees of longitude and latitude still to go nauseate me. Dreary, hectic day (I'm writing this on the plane taking me to Porto Alegre). At 11 o'clock, a visit from some Brazilian philosophers, who've come to ask me for a couple of "clarifications." Lunch with a young couple, French professors. Charming. Then a visit to the Alliance Française. Stroll with Mme. P. through the streets of São Paulo, where I come across a photo of myself that humbles me. Cocktail at Valeur. Dinner at Sylvestre's. A talk. The lecture hall is again overflowing, with some people standing. A kind Frenchwoman brought me some Gauloises. After the talk, I'm taken to a theater to hear a Brazilian singer. Then champagne at Andrade's. I return totally worn out, tired of the human face.

*

August 9

Leave for Porto Alegre, Andrade and Sylvestre are emotional, etc. Lunch on the plane. For the first time, a little coughing fit. But nobody notices. In Porto Alegre, I disembark into a biting cold. Four or five frozen French people are waiting for me at the airport. They tell me I have to give a talk that evening, which isn't something we'd agreed to. Saw some capotes[47]—The light is quite beautiful. The city ugly. Despite its five rivers. These islets of civilization are often hideous. In the evening, the talk. They have to turn people away. The press exaggerates the whole thing. That rather amuses me, though. My main concern is to get going and to finish, to finish this once and for all. They realize I don't have a visa for Chile. We have to stop in Montevideo, telegraph, etc.

*

August 10

Stroll in the city. Plane at 2:00 P.M., where I'm writing this and what preceded it. Terrible sadness and feeling of isolation. My mail hasn't caught up with me and I'm moving farther away from it.

The welcome given by the French officials in Montevideo lacks warmth. The dates for my talks have already been changed several times. Though I had nothing to do with it. They even neglected to reserve a room for me. I end up in a sort of comfortless storage room—where, all the same, I feel better than in the company of my forced hosts. It takes me a while to fall asleep, tossing and turning, focusing my willpower on not falling to pieces before the end of the trip.

Forced to admit to myself that, for the first time in my life, I'm in the midst of a psychological meltdown. That stable poise that's withstood everything else has now collapsed, despite all my effort. Murky waters inside me, hazy shapes passing in them, sapping all my energy. This depression is hell, so to speak. If the people welcoming me here could only feel the

47 In the original manuscript, the word is hard to make out, though it seems reasonable that Camus was referring to "capotes," the warm, poncho-like coats worn in the region.

effort I'm making just to appear normal, they'd at least make an effort to smile.

*

August 11

Get up early, write some letters. Then, still without news from my chaperones, I go out into a beautiful, icy day in Montevideo. The tip of the city is bathed in the yellow waters of the Rio de la Plata. Spacious and orderly, Montevideo is surrounded by a necklace of beaches and a maritime boulevard that seems beautiful. There's a relaxed quality to this city, which seems easier to live in than the others I've seen here. Mimosas in the beachfront neighborhoods, palm trees reminiscent of Menton. Relieved, also, to be in a Spanish-speaking country. Return to my room. My chaperones are waking up. I'll leave by boat this evening, from Rio de la Plata to Buenos Aires. Lunch at the attaché's. Quai d'Orsay and flowery nonsense. He's a good guy, nonetheless. In the evening, the boat leaves Montevideo. I again gaze at the moon on the silty waters—but my heart is colder now than it was on the *Campana*.

*

August 12

In the morning, Buenos Aires. Huge cluster of houses pushing outward. W.R. is waiting for me. We discuss the matter of giving talks. I hold my ground, adding that my talk, if I were to give it, would focus in part on freedom of expression. Given, moreover, that he assumes the censor would be able to request a transcript of the talk to be read ahead of time, I warn him that I would categorically refuse. He's of the opinion, then, that it would be best not to go looking for trouble before it finds you. Same with the ambassador. Tour of the city—a rare degree of ugliness. Lot of people in the afternoon. Finally, I get to V.O.'s.[48] Nice, large house like the kind in *Gone with the Wind.* Grand, old luxury. I'd like to lie down and sleep there until the end of the world. I do drift off to sleep, in fact.

*

August 13

Good night. I wake to a cold and foggy day. V. sends me letters from her room. Then the papers. The Peronist press quietly ignored or softened the statements I made yesterday afternoon. Lunch with the editor of *Prensa* (opposition), the police beat, etc. Afternoon, forty people. After getting out of that, dinner with V. and we talk until midnight. She has me listen to Britten's *Rape of Lucretia* and the recorded poems of Baudelaire—very nice. First real night of relaxation since I set out. I'd like to stay here until it's time to go back home—to avoid the continual struggle that drains all my energy. There's a temporary peace in this house.

*

August 14

At 9 o'clock, no news of the plane that's supposed to take me to Chile. At 12 o'clock, we call. Day spent at V's waiting to depart.

48 Victoria Ocampo (V.O.) (1890–1979)—Argentinian writer and founder of the influential literary magazine *Sur.* She first approached Camus after his talk at Columbia University in 1946. *Sur* had just published a translation of *Caligula.* In 1953, when Ocampo was arrested for her anti-Perónist political positions, Camus sent a letter, signed by a group of well-known French writers, to the Argentinian ambassador demanding her release.

Rafael Alberti[49] is there, with his wife. Likeable. I know he's a communist. I end up explaining my point of view to him. He agrees with me. But some slander will eventually come to separate me from this man who is and should remain a comrade. What's to be done?[50] We're in the age of separation. The plane finally takes off, at sunset. We pass over the Andes at night— and I can't see a thing—which just about sums up the trip. If anything, I glimpse a few snowy ridges in the night. But before night had completely fallen, I had the chance to see the immense and monotonous pampas—which have no end. The descent on Santiago happens in a flash, through a velvety sky, with a forest of winking stars at our feet. The gentle caress of these cities stretched out along the ocean at night.

*

August 15

On the Pacific with Charvet and Fron. Ch. tells me how earthquakes influence the way Chileans comport themselves. Five hundred shocks a year—several of them catastrophic. It creates a psychology of instability. Chileans are gamblers, spending everything they have and doing politics day by day.

We ride on: the long white breakers riding atop the Pacific. Santiago huddled between the water and the Andes. Intense colors (marigolds the color of rust), the blossoming plum and

---

49 Rafael Alberti Merello (1902–99)—Spanish Surrealist poet and dramaturge.

50 The phrase "Que faire?" ("What's to be done?") is as common in French as it is in English, which makes it hard to know if Camus is winking at Lenin's famous pamphlet bearing the same title. That said, the phrase is used only twice in the South American journals, and in both cases it follows talk of either Communism or the Soviet Union.

almond trees etched against a white background of snowy peaks—an admirable country.

Afternoon: drudgery. At six o'clock, a forum. I'm feeling good. Dinner at Charvet's. I'm in the midst of depression. I drink too much, due to exhaustion, and don't get to sleep until late. Time lost.

*

August 16

Hellish day. Radio, sightseeing. Lunch with Vincent Anidobre's son[51] in a little house at the foot of the Andes. Colloquium with the local theater people. At 7 o'clock, a talk in a room so packed it's exhausting.[52] Dinner at the embassy, a flood of boredom. Only the ambassador is amusing; yesterday, he took his jacket off and danced.

*

August 17

Day of unrest and riots. Protests were already taking place yesterday. But today it feels like an earthquake. The cause: an increase in the "micro" fare (Santiago's subway system). Buses are overturned and burned. Glass is shattered on the ones that

51 Probably Vincente Garcia-Huidobro Portales (1916–?), the elder son of the celebrated Chilean poet Vincente Huidobro (1893–1948). The senior Huidobro was a prominent figure in the post–World War I literary vanguard in Paris and Madrid who introduced contemporary European, especially French, innovations in poetic form and imagery to Chile.

52 On August 16, Camus gave his "Time of the Murderers" talk at the University of Chile. On August 17, as he notes here, his talk on Chamfort was moved to the French Institute owing to unrest at the university.

pass through. In the afternoon, I'm told that the university, where the students protested, is closed—and that my talk won't be able to take place there. Within two hours, the French department has arranged for a talk at the French Institute. When I leave there, the shops have lowered their gates and the armed-and-helmeted troops literally occupy the city. They fire a blank every now and then. It's a state of emergency.[53] During the night, I hear shots fired here and there.

*

August 18

Plane delayed until nighttime. Bad weather in the Andes. I sleep poorly here, if at all—and I'm tired. The Charvets[54] come get me at 11 o'clock, and I'm asleep on my feet. That's how bad my night went. But their kindness isn't a burden, and we drive through the Chilean countryside. Mimosa trees and weeping willows. Beautiful, hearty nature. At our next stop, an excellent lunch in front of an open fire. Then, we branch off toward the Andes and stop for a bite in a mountain lodge, in front of a beautiful fire, once again. I'm doing well in Chile and I could see myself living here for a little while, if circumstances were different. When we get back, we learn that the plane won't be ready until the next morning. The rain's coming down in buckets. Dinner at the Charvets'. Bed at midnight. At the hotel, I find some parting gifts. It takes me a long time to fall asleep.

*

53 Here, Camus uses the term "l'état de siège," the title he had given to his 1948 play about the arrival of the plague in Cádiz, Spain.
54 The Charvets were a French couple living in Chile who hosted Camus during his stay in 1949.

August 19

At 4:30 A.M., the company calls. I'm to be at the airfield at 6 o'clock. At 7:00 A.M., the plane takes off. But then, after it seemed the path had been set, the plane heads south and follows another path, after having gone 200 km out of the way. The Andes: prodigious, shattered ranges tearing through mountains of clouds—but the snow is dazzling. We're constantly pitching and rolling, and to make matters worse, I have a coughing fit. I just manage to avoid the worst—and pretend to be asleep.

We don't reach Buenos Aires until noon. By that point, the lack of sleep overwhelms me. V.O. came to get me but nobody from the embassy came and they also haven't gotten me a ticket to Montevideo, though I have a talk there at 6:30 P.M. Thanks to V., we hustle to Buenos Aires, then to the seaplane airport. There are no open seats. V. telephones a friend. Everything is taken care of. I leave at 4:45 P.M., the weather bad, a yellow sky over yellow waters. At 5:45, Montevideo. The embassy sent someone to tell me they decided to cancel the talk and to take me to the French high school instead. There, the principal tells me that some people have shown up anyway and that he doesn't know what to do. I suggest a debate, even though I'm running on empty. They agree and reschedule my two talks for the next day, one at 11:00 A.M., the other at 6:00 P.M. Debate. Then to bed, drunk with exhaustion.

*

August 20

Brutal day. At 10:00 A.M., journalists and C. At 11:00 A.M., first talk, in a hall at the University. In the middle of the talk, a curious character enters the hall. A cape, a short beard, a cold look in the eye. He finds himself a spot at the back, standing up, opens a journal and ostensibly reads it. From time to time, he coughs loudly. At least the guy livens up the auditorium. A minute with José Bergamín,[55] a refined man with the worn, deeply lined face of a Spanish intellectual. He doesn't want to choose between Catholicism and Communism until the Spanish Civil War is over. A hypotensive man whose energy is solely spiritual. My kind of guy.

Bergamín: my deepest temptation is suicide. A dramatic suicide. (Return to Spain at the risk of being jailed, resist, and die.)

Lunch with some nice couples, French professors. At 4 o'clock, press conference. At 5 o'clock, I see the director of the theater that's going to stage *Caligula*. He wants to throw in some ballet. It's all the rage internationally. At 6 o'clock, Mlle. Lussitch and the charming cultural attaché from Uruguay take me for a short ride through the gardens near the city limits. The evening is gentle, quick, and a little tender. This country is beautiful and easygoing. I'm able to relax a little. At 6:30, the second talk. The ambassador felt obliged to come with his better half. In the first row, the sinister faces of boredom and vulgarity. After the talk, I go for a walk with Bergamín. We end up in a packed café. He doubts the effectiveness of what he's doing. I tell him that maintaining an uncompromising refusal is a positive act, with positive consequences—Then dinner at Suzannah Soca's. A crowd of society women who, after a third whisky, become a little much. A couple of them literally offer themselves to me—but that's not such a compliment. A Frenchwoman standing right in front of me finds a way to be an apologist for Franco. Exhausted, I go for it—and then realize I'd

---

55 José Bergamín (1895–1983)—Spanish writer and antifascist activist who went into exile in Latin America and France after Franco's victory.

better take my leave. I ask the cultural attaché if she'd like to come have a drink with me, and we make our escape. At least this pretty face makes it easier to live. The night hangs gentle over Montevideo. A clear sky, the rustling of dry palm leaves above the Place de la Constitution, flights of pigeons, white in the black sky. The hour would be relaxing, and this solitude I feel, without news for 18 days, without confidence, might be eased, but then the charming attaché begins to recite for me, in the middle of the square, some French poems she's written, miming their tragic nature, arms thrust out at her sides, voice rising and falling.[56] I sit tight. Then we go for a drink and I take her home. I go to bed and the anxiety and melancholy return, keeping me from sleeping.

*

August 21

Up at 8:00 A.M. I slept 3 or 4 hours But the plane takes off at 11 o'clock. Beneath a tender sky, freshly fluffed and cloudy, Montevideo unfurls its beaches—a charming city where everything requires happiness—and a witless happiness. Stupidity of traveling by plane—a retrograde and barbaric way of getting around. At 5 o'clock, we're flying over Rio, and on descent, I'm greeted by that dense and humid air, its consistency like cotton wool, which I'd forgotten about and which is particular to Rio. The garish, multicolored parrots, too, and a peacock

56 Four days earlier, on August 16, Camus wrote to Maria Casarès: "It's been fourteen days since I heard from you and I don't know if you can imagine what that means to me. I want to believe with all my strength that my mail's been held up in Rio for reasons I don't understand, but I can't help imagining, sometimes, that maybe you haven't written to me, and then I sink into a state it would be better not to tell you about." Camus and Casarès, *Correspondance*, 155–56.

with a discordant voice. Barely able to get to bed, with no news, not a single piece of mail waiting for me at the embassy.

*

August 22

My mail is brought to me. It's been sitting around in some office for 18 days. Tired, I don't leave my room all day. In the evening, a talk, after which a drink with Mme. Mineur. To bed with a fever.

*

August 23

Get up a little better. My departure approaches. It'll be Thursday or Saturday. I think of Paris as of a monastery. Lunch in Copacabana, in front of the sea. The waves are high and gentle. Watching them calms me down a little. Back to my room. I sleep a little. At 5 o'clock, public debate session with Brazilian students. Is it the fatigue? I've never felt so loose and easy. Dinner at the Claveries' with Mme. R., a ravishing woman, but without much depth, it seems.

*

August 24

I get up a little better still. Departure is now set for Saturday. Sightseeing in the morning and the exhaustion returns. So much so I decide not to have lunch. At 1:30, Pedrosa[57] and his

57 Mário Pedrosa (1900–1981)—Brazilian art critic and public intellectual known for his pivotal role in establishing Brazilian modernism. A Marxist working at the intersection of art and politics, Pedrosa was a columnist for two Rio newspapers, *Correio da Manhã* and *Jornal do Brasil*.

wife come get me so we can go see some paintings done by the insane, out in the banlieues, in a hospital of modern lines and ancient grime. It's heartbreaking to see faces behind those tall window bars. Two interesting painters. The others surely have what it takes to send our forward-thinking Parisians into fits of rapture—but what they have, in fact, is ugliness. Even more striking in the sculptures, ugly and vulgar. It terrifies me to recognize that one of the institution's young psychiatric doctors is the boy who, at the beginning of the trip, asked me the most asinine question anyone has asked me in all of South America. He's the one deciding the fate of these unfortunate people. Quite touched himself, really. But I'm even more terrified when he tells me he'll be making the trip to Paris with me on Saturday; 36 hours locked up in a metal box with him, that's the final straw.

In the evening, dinner at Pedrosa's with some intelligent people. Pouring rain on the way back.

*

August 25

Flu. Clearly, this climate doesn't agree with me. I work a little in the morning, then go to the zoo to see the sloth.

The sloth is free-roaming and you have to try to find it among the park's thousands of trees. I give up. At least the leopards are splendid—the lizards terrible and the anteater, too. Lunch with Letarget in Copacabana. Rio is veiled in an incessant rain that pools in the holes of the pavement and sidewalk, dissolving the thin veneer they've used to try to cover up the problem. The colonial city shows through, and I have to say that it's much more attractive like this, covered in mud, trampled over, its sky filled with mist. Shopping in the afternoon. Everything I find in this country comes from somewhere else. In the evening, at 5 o'clock, Mendès's place. Another crazy crowd, where I'm bored and no longer have the strength to hide it. Physically, I can no longer bear large gatherings. Same thing at dinner, where there were seven of us when I thought it would be only Pedrosa and Barleto, where everyone cuts each other off while speaking, and at the top of their voice, too. Fueled by my flu, the ordeal becomes hellish. I'd like to go back, but I don't dare let them know. At 1:00 A.M., Mme. Pedrosa notices that I can barely keep myself upright, and I go to bed.[58]

*

August 26 and 27

Two awful days dragging about with my flu, to different places with different people, numb to all I see, concerned only with regaining my strength, amid people who, in their friendship or hysterics, notice nothing of the state I'm in and so make it that much worse. Evening at the consul's where I hear comments about the necessity of corporal punishment in our colonial armies.

Saturday 4:00 P.M. I'm informed that the plane's motor has broken down and the plane won't be leaving until tomorrow, Sunday. The fever's getting worse and I'm beginning to wonder if it's not something more than the flu.

*

58 On August 21, Camus wrote to Maria Casarès: "For eighteen days I've fought the fatigue, a frightful depression that's gotten worse, the sleepless nights, exhausting work, the crowds of people who speak, challenge, ask, pressure … This trip has been exhausting. Plane, talk, reception, journalists, hysterical society women, and then the wholeting over again the next day." Camus and Casarès, *Correspondance*, 157–58.

August 31

Sick. Bronchitis, at the least. They call to tell me we'll be leaving this afternoon. Glorious day. Doctor. Penicillin. The trip finishes in a metal coffin, between a mad doctor and a diplomat, heading for Paris.

"Absurdiste," New Yorker, April 20, 1946, "Talk of the Town"

Albert Camus, the young French author, is over here for a few lectures and the appearance of his novel, "The Stranger."[1]

He has an idea for a daily newspaper that would take a lot of the fun out of newspapering. "It would be a critical newspaper, to be published one hour after the first editions of the other papers, twice a day, morning and evening," he told us when we called on him in a hotel on West Seventieth Street, where he had spent his first five days in America. "It would evaluate the probable element of trash in the other papers' main stories, with due regard to editorial policies and the past performance of the correspondents. Once equipped with card-indexed dossiers on the correspondents, a critical newspaper would work very fast. After a few weeks the whole tone of the press would conform more closely to reality. An international service." M. Camus, who is thirty-two and dresses like a character in "Harold Teen," retired six months ago as editor-in-chief of *Combat*, a Paris daily he directed during the German occupation, when it was extra-legal. In the first year following the Liberation, he made *Combat* the most interesting inde-

---

1 This article is reproduced courtesy of Christina Carver Pratt and the St. Clair McKelway Estate.

pendent journal in France. *Combat* now, he thinks, has passed
from independence to a simple habit of negation, which isn't
the same thing.

For the time being, Camus is more interested in further novels, his play "Caligula," which has been bought for New York
production, and his philosophy of the absurd than he is in
journalism. He is often called an existentialist, like his friend
Jean-Paul Sartre, but he says he is not. His philosophy is not
the same thing at all as Sartre's, whose disciples, he says, are im-
pressed with the consciousness of existence, which is to them
at times a mystic pleasure and rather more often a pain in
the neck. What burns Camus is the necessity to stop existing.
He believes man's relation to the universe is absurd because
man must die. But he also believes that acceptance of this relation is the mark of maturity. Sisyphus, who was condemned
to roll a rock up a hill in Hades and then see it roll down again,
is Camus's symbol: he knew what he was up against, but he
kept on pushing. For a man arrived at such a grim conclusion,
Camus seemed unduly cheerful, as did, in fact, M. Sartre when
he was here some weeks ago. "Just because you have pessimistic thoughts, you don't have to act pessimistic," Camus said.
"One has to pass the time somehow. Look at Don Juan." He
despises the kind of "realism" that confounds greatness with
strength and material success; the dangerous part he took in
the Resistance was an assertion of his disagreement with this
concept. When we saw him, he was looking at the translation
of "The Stranger" for the first time. "There are too many quotation marks in it," he said. "I'm sure there weren't that many
quotation marks in the original."

Camus has a snub-nosed face that looks more Spanish than
French. His mother, who was born in Algeria, was of Spanish blood. His father, also born in Algeria, belonged to one of
the Alsatian families that moved there after the war of 1870–

1871 rather than become German.[2] Camus was born in Algiers himself, and is, we got him to admit without too much trouble, the first top-notch French writer born in North Africa. His birth there gave him a distinctive chemistry, because the European cities in French North Africa are as new and ruthlessly commercial as Birmingham or Detroit. They have their color problems, with accompanying overtones of guilt; their competing immigrant strains (Camus's parentage combines two); and their savage and explicit anti-Semitism (the proportion of Jews to Christians is much higher than in Continental France). They also have their crude and desperate first or second-generation millionaires who have never learned that it sometimes pays to be reasonable. The summers are extreme, like New York's. Camus graduated from the University of Algiers and moved to France only in 1940.

The thing that bothered him about France at first was the oversupply of historic and literary associations. "What the heart craves, at certain moments, is places without poetry," he once wrote. West Seventieth Street ought to suit him fine.

2 Editor's note: Camus's mother, Catherine Sintès Camus, was still living in 1946. Camus believed that his father, who died when he was an infant, had Alsatian roots. In fact, his paternal great-grandfather Claude, a native of Bordeaux, was among the first settlers in Algeria in the 1840s.

Close-up, New York Post, June 5, 1946

"I Revolt—We Are!" by Dorothy Norman

Direct, unaffected, forceful, Albert Camus has captured the imagination of advance-guard literary circles in America.[1] As France's most talented young writer to emerge from the "resistance" period, he has had a warm welcome from many in this country.

Editor of the French underground newspaper *Combat* during the long months of Nazi occupation, Camus has abandoned journalism for a series of highly significant volumes, already exerting world-wide influence.

At the first question currently asked of every young French author—"Are you an existentialist?"—Camus shudders. He has a horror of systems. "You can explain nothing by way of principles and ideologies," he firmly declares.

Claiming that despair and mere anguish play much too great a role in such contemporary philosophical schools of thought as "existentialism," Camus feels that we will solve our problems through active revolt rather than through negativism.

That his own philosophy is one of revolt is not a matter of mere words. It is proved not only by the active position he took against fascism both before and during the war, but by

---

1 This article is reproduced courtesy of the *New York Post.*

the themes he has chosen to develop in his books, as, for example, in "The Stranger," written and published in France several years ago and just issued in America by Alfred Knopf.

"What is generally misunderstood," he explains, "is that when the word revolt is used, it is generally supposed to imply romanticism—as of a Byron, or one or another form of Marxism. But revolt can be much more modest in its implications."

Not the Skyscrapers, The Bowery, Moved Him

The hero of "The Stranger," he explains, is simply "a man who refuses to lie. That is the sum and substance of his meaning. The book's second meaning is that society apparently thinks that what it needs is men who are willing to give only superficial signs of their feelings. If a man dares to say what he truly feels, if he revolts against having to lie, then society will destroy him in the end. "The Stranger" is a story of a sincere man against that kind of world." And it is against that kind of world that Camus feels we must revolt. Each of us. Not a mere abstraction of us. But each of us—in every act. Not in some "other world" either. But in this one. Now. This moment.

Camus himself is a modest man. You feel it in everything he says. You feel it in the way he comments on New York. It is not our skyscrapers that have moved him, but our Bowery. He likes our literature of the 19th century—Melville and Henry James—better, so far, than what he has read of the 20th century. You feel it in the way he dresses. The relaxed tweed suit. You feel it in the way he speaks. There is no philosophical jargon.

One thing that has struck him on the favorable side in America is the extraordinary feeling he has, as a European, to be permitted to wander about freely—without being asked for marks of identification. Despite this freedom, however, he shakes his head sadly in contemplating the ignominious way in which we treat the Negro. That he was disturbed by our attitude on this score—as are most Europeans—even before he reached our shores, was evidenced, for example, when he took upon himself the responsibility of seeing that the works of Richard Wright were translated and published in Paris.

That Man Who Rolled The Stone Uphill!

"I wonder," he ponders, "whether despite the apparent energy and youth of America, due to the crisis through which Europe has passed, we Europeans have not something to give to America after all. I refer, of course, to [*sic*] sense of disquiet.

"It is important to be disquieted. It is tremendously important. We are pressed for time. Maturity is needed fast. We have no time to waste."

Born in the department of Constantine, Camus was brought to Algiers at the age of five months, where he lived until he left for France to work in journalism—in 1938.[2] He received his education in communal public school in Algiers, winning a scholarship at the age of ten, holding twelve jobs while pursuing his studies, and developing an interest in philosophy while still quite young.

His father died in 1914 when Camus was still a baby; his family was very poor; his mother worked steadily and diligently to support him and his brother while they were growing up. His plans for the future?

He has been eagerly talking to students and other young people in America and making contact with those who have an international feeling about the interdependence of man. In his search—as in his work—he is less concerned with finding

2 Editor's note: Camus moved to France to work at *Paris-Soir* in March 1940.

some theological or rational reason why mankind should move forward together than with the moving forward itself. What moves him is the Greek myth of Sisyphus, waging a surely losing fight against logic, perpetually rolling a huge stone to the top of a hill despite the fact that he not only never completely reaches the top, but the stone inevitably rolls back again.

His own philosophical position is one which goes beyond the traditional rationalistic philosophy of a Descartes. Here is how he sums it up: "Descartes said, "I doubt; therefore I think; therefore I am." As for myself I substitute for Descartes' 'I doubt' the realization that from a rationalistic point of view the world is 'absurd.' Because it is 'absurd' instead of saying 'I think' I say 'I revolt.' If I revolt this means not 'I am' but 'we are.' In other words, my revolt involves not simply myself but man."

Fourth Phase of Work Will Be on Love

These three phases of his philosophy will eventually be revealed in three phases of his work as now planned: that of 'absurdity' is characteristic of such a book as "The Stranger," the second phase is reflected in his subsequent work on man's revolt; the third will be represented by a novel, an essay, and a play, based on the concept of "we are." "And then what?" I asked. "Then," he smiled, "there will be a fourth phase in which I shall write a book about love."

Of the work already completed, in addition to "The Stranger," there are such volumes as "The Myth of Sisyphus," "Caligula," "Letters to a German Friend."

Camus' decision to give up journalism in order to devote himself completely to his writing is a decisive one. It isn't easy to support a wife and two children on that basis in the France of today—especially when you refuse "to compromise or to popularize."

But despite his fragile health, Camus is a determined young man with a mission. You cannot help feel his very modesty and sense of dedication will carry him far.

Acknowledgments

Editor's Acknowledgments

My thanks go to Ryan Bloom for our in-depth exchanges and for his important contributions to the notes. Livia Bokor's research and criticism were essential. Thanks Adam Gopnik for *New Yorker* history and to Etienne Sauthier for photo research. I benefited from Alexandre Alajbegovic's good counsel at every phase. My deepest thanks go to Catherine Camus and Elisabeth Maisondieu-Camus for their guardianship of Albert Camus's legacy and for their generosity. Finally, to our discerning editors, Alan Thomas, Randy Petilos, and Dylan Montanari, grateful thanks.

Translator's Acknowledgments

Thank you to Alice Kaplan, for our many discussions on the finer points of these pages, and to Christen Aragoni, for her close reading of the translation. Thanks also to The Corporation of Yaddo and the English Department at the University of Maryland, Baltimore County, both of which, in their own way, allowed me the time to complete this project.

Index

Note: Page numbers in italics refer to figures.